# TEACHING CHILDREN
## Laying Foundations for Faith

By
Chris Ward
David Morrow
Anne Tonks

PHOTO CREDITS

S & W Productions:
    pp. 10,18,19,23,25,26,31,34,47,53,57,59,73,86,89,97,111,114
The Stock Market:
    pp. 9,11,14,15,21,37,40,41,48,50,62,70,71,76,83,90,94,98,102,107,123,129,132

# Writers

## Chris Ward

Chris Ward has loved and taught children for twenty-five years. She currently is a professor of education at Trevecca College in Nashville, Tennessee. Chris holds a Doctor of Education in Curriculum and Supervision from Peabody College of Vanderbilt University, a Masters in Education from Peabody College, and a Bachelor's of Science from Western Kentucky University in Bowling Green. Chris teaches first graders in Sunday School. Chris and her husband, Tom, have three children, Jenny, Amanda, and Josh; and one grandson, Blaine.

## David Morrow

David Morrow is the director of the Children's Sunday School Ministry Department at LifeWay Christian Resources. David is a graduate of Mississippi College and Southwestern Baptist Theological Seminary. David has served as a minister of education and minister of childhood education and a state preschool/children's consultant for Mississippi. David teaches third graders in Sunday School. David and his wife, Amy, have three daughters, Jennifer, Heather, and Stacy; and one grandson, Coleman David.

## Anne Tonks

Anne Tonks, manager of the Children's Ministry Services Section in the Children's Sunday School Ministry Department at LifeWay, has written for and worked with children for fifty years. She is a native of Canada and a graduate of the University of Louisville and Indiana University. For the past twenty-three years, she has served at LifeWay Christian Resources as a children's editor, consultant, and ministry designer. Anne serves as Children's Division Outreach Director. Anne has three sons, Doug, Ken, and Stephen; and one grandson, Andrew.

# Contents

# Foreword

Captioned beneath a photograph of a girl examining a world globe in her school classroom was this question: "Is her Bible study changing the way she approaches her studies and conducts herself in the classroom?" It's a question every children's Sunday School leader needs to ask and answer.

Even with the proliferation of Bible study groups, a startling level of biblical illiteracy exists among believers. Many ignore biblical authority and are only nominally obedient to God. The way they live is not significantly different from the way non-believers live.

To affect change we must teach for *spiritual transformation*.

*Spiritual transformation* is God's work of changing a believer into the likeness of Jesus by creating a new identity in Christ and by empowering a lifelong relationship of love, trust, and obedience to glorify God. Teaching for *spiritual transformation* is concerned with helping people live to make a difference in the world around them.

In traveling across America the past five years, I have met many people whose lives have been transformed through an encounter with God's Word. One was a business executive who was willing to unload a truckload of pipe himself so his Sunday School teacher could share the gospel with the truck owner. Another was a mother in Boston who voluntarily served in several churches in the New England area because she was so moved by their needs. A third was a teacher in Texas who left the comfort of her own growing church to teach the Bible in a struggling inner-city mission.

These people heard a Bible lesson, but they didn't stop there. They continued to interact with God's Truth, allowing it to change their lives.

Teaching for *spiritual transformation* will yield thousands of believers who will give their best service to Christ. Then when we are confronted with questions like the one above, we can reply: "Yes. Her Bible study is changing the way she approaches her studies and conducts herself in the classroom, because the Truth she encounters in Scripture is changing her life."

Bill L. Taylor, Director
Sunday School Group

Jesus went throughout Galilee, teaching in their synagogues, preaching the good news of the kingdom, and healing every disease and sickness among the people. Matthew 4:23

# Chapter 1

# Teaching As Jesus Taught

## By David Morrow

I have often wondered what it would have been like to have been one of Jesus' followers sitting on the mountainside as He talked about what we call the Beatitudes.

How might I have felt if I had been the young boy sitting, listening, learning? How might I have felt when I was given the opportunity to practice my faith by giving up my lunch of bread and fish?

I have tried to imagine what it would have been like to be near Jesus; to have heard Him pray, seen His miracles, and learned from the Great Teacher.

### Jesus as Relationship Builder

Everyone around Jesus, from the most trusted followers to those who wished to see him dead, recognized Him as Teacher. The most common way of addressing Jesus in the New Testament was *lord*. The second most common was *rabbi* or *teacher*. Even today those who deny His deity, acknowledge that He was a great Teacher.

Jesus has for eternity been set above all others as King of kings and Lord of lords. No less than the Creator of the universe has provided His Son Jesus as the living example and more. But what was it about Jesus that set Him apart from other teachers? Were His methods radical? Was His message new? One thing that set Jesus apart was the clarity and compassion with which he taught the message of the Kingdom of God.

Volumes have been written about Jesus and how He taught. Truly His teaching could be gathered around one central element: relationships. It was as true in the time of Jesus as it is today: relationships are preeminent in teaching. One cannot really be a teacher unless he has learners. Jesus worked at developing relationships with his learners. The primary investment of Jesus' life and the Kingdom message was through the deepest relationships with His disciples. Those 12 men developed deep relationships and understanding through spending time together. Through daily interaction, the disciples grew to know Jesus not only from what He said, but also from how He lived. That relationship can be likened to today's deepest, greatest investment of time, our families.

Parents (and persons who have a custodial responsibility in a family-type relationship) recognize the value and challenge of teaching by example. Children learn best when spoken teachings are lived out in flesh-and-blood examples. There is no question in my mind that we must move into this next century recognizing that children are at the crossroads, and it will be the seven-day-a-week lessons that will make the crucial difference in their lives. Teachers as well as parents with children still at home need to be vigilant in learning from Jesus, teaching by example, and modeling the Bible truths for the children.

The next level of relationship Jesus exhibited was with the followers who eagerly sought Him whenever and wherever He was accessible as He taught, worshiped, and traveled around the countryside. Most people had either heard of Him or perhaps had been among the

crowds that regularly gathered when He taught. The gatherings were informal and the people instantly found comfort in Jesus' words. Questions about the real meaning of the Kingdom of God that many had had since childhood were being answered before their very eyes.

That level of relationship may be something like the relationship you have with the teachers and children in your Sunday School department. You don't live together, but you have a regular association, so there is a developing depth to the relationship. The crowds pushed closer and followed longer to learn more about the Teacher and what He had to say about God.

Jesus' ministry to that group of people was significant. Many from the group became the foundation for the young church in the book of Acts. Those followers learned a great deal because Jesus met them at their level of understanding and brought them one step closer each time they were with Him. He told them stories that related to their lives and lovingly cared for their needs.

## The Teacher as a Relationship Builder

Children's teachers have a unique role in much the same way. The blending of friend and teacher, minister and mentor leads to a very full job description. One of the joys and challenges of teaching is that the role requires all one has to offer. The New Testament reminds us that Jesus felt the need to be alone, but the crowds sought Him out. He never turned them away. He invested Himself in those who needed Him.

Over the decades of the recent past, thousands of children who would never have been encouraged to accept Christ by their parents have been reached by caring

churches—churches with teachers who discovered the children not attending any church and encouraged them to participate in church activities. Many teachers even picked the children up in their own cars so that they could attend church. Other churches had aggressive outreach plans that reached entire families through Vacation Bible School. More recently, many churches provided some kind of transportation for children to attend church, such as buses or vans. All these methods provide opportunities for Christian adults to build relationships with children and families who, like the crowds around Jesus, found comfort in loving, compassionate arms.

The last group of people to be influenced by the teachings of Jesus could not be called disciples. Some were curious, uninvolved onlookers, perhaps there just for what they would receive. Others were His enemies, those who were opposed to all that Jesus said and did. But even for those people, Jesus still met their needs and touched their lives through relationships with them.

## Why Jesus Used Different Teaching Approaches

Jesus was always a teacher, even when He was not in the temple or synagogue. He was a teacher in the comfort of a friend's home, on the side of a mountain, and in a boat on the Sea of Galilee. Around little children, with the blind or lame, with His closest friends or with challengers,.Jesus was always teaching

Children's leaders, too, are teachers in every act of every day. People all around notice and are influenced by the things that we say—good or bad.

Jesus taught in different ways because people learn in different ways. When teaching children at church, leaders intentionally look for different ways to teach them. Teachers know that it is easier to grasp the message if the method is interesting or engaging for the learner. Jesus knew that people approached understanding from different perspectives.

## The Purpose of Jesus' Teaching

Jesus' entire life was purpose driven. He was born, God in human flesh, for a specific purpose, and He lived His life out in fulfillment of that purpose. His purpose was to proclaim the Kingdom of God. His teaching was to guide His followers to an understanding of what the Kingdom of God meant. Jesus guided followers to an understanding of the Kingdom through the renewing of their minds.

Renewal leads to transformation. Spiritual transformation is still the heart of our purpose. We still seek to guide children to understand the Kingdom of God through a relationship with Jesus Christ. A spiritual relationship with Jesus requires that we give up our own will in life in exchange for God's will—to become "living sacrifices" (Rom. 12:1). I fear that for some, Bible study has lost that passion. It has become routine, a habit, an obligation; but with no life transformation.

Jesus was so passionate about His calling that He gave His entire being to it. He did not work in the carpenter shop and once in a while tell stories. He did not ask the fishermen to give Him only their Sabbaths. Rather He committed Himself fully to the task, and called His disciples to leave their profession, their source of income, and follow Him.

Think about how radical, how passionate, how committed they were to the task. I wonder if in today's world Jesus asks us to have that kind of commitment. I wonder if Jesus wants me to teach my third graders with the excitement and passion that those men shared with those around them.

Teachers must see their teaching task as a commitment to more than just caring for children while parents are in a Bible study meeting. They must see their departments and classes and the children in those departments and classes as Jesus would see them. With a commitment of love and compassion, teachers invest in the future by helping more boys and girls understand the Bible that

---

Resources produced for children by the Southern Baptist Convention help teachers read the Bible passage and gain an understanding of it. The studies guide the teacher toward a transformational experience, building a relationship with God, that she can share with the children in the Bible study time.

Think about the level of your own commitment. On a scale of one to five (five being the highest), how would you rate yourself?

1    2    3    4    5

Think of some ways in which you might increase your commitment to Christ.

will lead to their own transformation. The Bible says that in Christ we are new creatures. We are literally helping children be reborn (John 3) into new creatures, too.

Are you teaching in a way that will best communicate and integrate the message into the lives of these young students? Or are you teaching in a way that is comfortable, a way in which you have taught for years, or maybe even a way that you were taught? That may not be all bad. But you may want to ask yourself the question, "Is there a better way?"

## Jesus and the Children

I have a friend who is a great sculptor. He has bronze statues in buildings all over the country. He has shared with

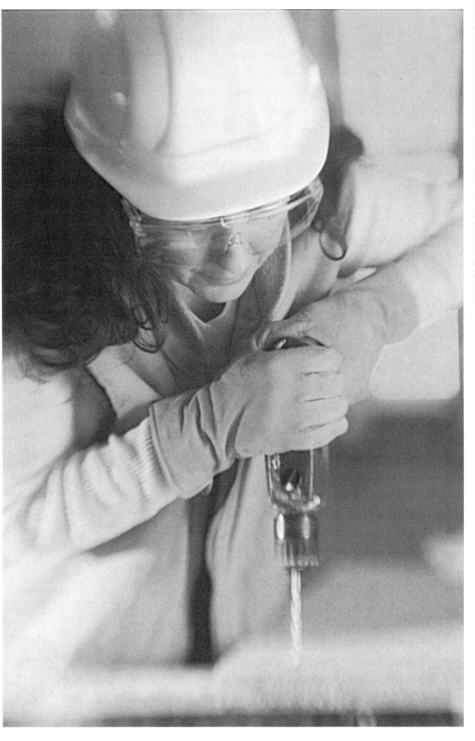

me an idea for a new piece that captures the spirit of Jesus and His relationship with children. My friend wants to make a life-size statue of Jesus sitting on a large rock. All around Him are children. You might think that the children would be in his arms and lap; but no. Instead, in the eyes of the artist, the bronze folds of Jesus' garment form a series of steps for today's children to climb up into Jesus' lap and sit on His knee. That is the heart of Jesus for children in Mark 10. He says, "Let the children come to me, for the kingdom of God belongs to them."

Christian adults can learn much from Jesus. He always had great compassion and love for everyone around Him. But in those instances when He interacted with children, there was a special tenderness. And Jesus clearly stated that there would be stiff consequences for anyone who caused a child to "stumble" (Matt. 18:6).

Teaching is a challenge, but the fruit of that labor is another generation of growing Christians. To teach as Jesus taught should be the goal of every children's worker. Such a goal will require the following:

- a current, ongoing relationship with the Master;
- studying the Word and spending time in prayer;
- considering each child's needs and learning styles
- planning for active involvement of the girls and boys throughout the session.

## My Challenge

Make the most of the time you have with the children you teach. Do not waste a single moment. Invest the minutes wisely. Much of that investment of time should be in building relationships. Some time will be spent in instruction, some in prayer and worship. Don't allow disorganization or lack of planning and preparation to diminish the time you have with the boys and girls.

In the book of James, chapter 3, the writer reminds teachers that we need to have a higher standard than others. As teachers of children, we must be vigilant because so much of what children learn may not be what we intended. The old truism, "It's more caught than taught", holds very true in the lives of the children we teach.

Look at the children around you. You will see in them your attitudes, your values, even your language reflected in their young lives. Children literally model their lives after the adults around them. My challenge to you is to be the kind of adult who models for boys and girls a life lived in the ways in which Christ lived. Remember this verse as your motto.

Do not conform any longer to the pattern of this world, but be transformed by the renewing of your mind.
Romans 12:2

And Jesus grew in wisdom and stature, and in favor with God and men. Luke 2:52

# Chapter 2

# The Children We Teach

## By Chris Ward

What do you think it is like to be a child today, at the dawning of a new century? Exciting? Scary? Stressful? Overwhelming? Children today face a myriad of challenges in their lives, and as teachers of children at church, we hear their stories.

Kendra reports that her parents are getting a divorce.

Antonio falls asleep in his chair because his mom must take him to work with her until midnight.

Tara asks for prayer because she is afraid someone in her school might bring a gun.

Lorenzo says he will not be in church for the next four Sundays because of his soccer tournaments.

The world today is one in which growing up seems to be more difficult than ever before. How are children and their families coping? In the past, it seems there may have been more coping mechanisms provided.

**The average child spends up to seven hours per day in front of the TV and only five minutes per day with Dad.**

Only 40 years ago, the culture in the home reflected a society that supported the family and its task of raising children. Children were more likely to grow up with both parents, stay at home until they were school age, and attend schools where teachers were valued. Family rituals were important; children ate meals and worshiped regularly with their families. The extended family lived in closer proximity, providing further spiritual and moral models for children.

Today's society has left the family to fend for itself in a world of personal freedom, independence, and tremendous mobility. The divorce rate is one in two and most Americans know only a few neighbors by name. Extended family members live farther away with less frequent contact and interaction. The majority of children need day care because of parental work demands. Fewer and fewer children share unhurried mealtimes with their families on a regular basis. More than ever, the role of the family is vital and irreplaceable. Our children desperately need family leadership and guidance, support and advice. And parents do not have to be alone during such turbulent times;

Teachers at church can help equip parents fulfill their responsibility as the primary Bible teachers and disciplers of their children.

The Sunday School principle of Family Responsibility affirms the home as the center of biblical guidance. It is all about putting first things first—God is the center of each family. Children need opportunities at home to hear Bible stories, sing hymns, participate in family Bible study and prayer. When parents spend time building spiritual foundations with their children, they show by word and deed the importance of God in their lives. Christian parents have the responsibility of guiding their children to integrate the Scriptures into their lives, thereby impacting how they think and act.

Katie is encouraged to spend some quiet time in her room each day talking to God, reading her daily devotionals, or listening to hymns and Christian music. When Pierce's mother tucks him in each night, she chooses a Scripture verse. Together they mark it in his Bible and talk about its meaning in his life.

Narquenta's family sets aside two nights a month for family worship. During the time, each family member shares prayer requests and leads a part of the worship.

Jacob's parents read the newsletters that come home from his teachers at church. Before he goes to Sunday School each week, Jacob's Mom or Dad has helped him mark in his Bible the memory verse and Bible story.

**Spiritual growth is a process that cannot be rushed and is as individual as each child. Spiritual foundations are built slowly and over time. During the childhood years, parents and teachers at church can work together to help a child fulfill God's plan for his life.**

## How Children Develop

In spite of the rapidly changing environment around them, children themselves have not changed. Children continue to develop and grow mentally, socially, emotionally, physically, and spiritually in predictable patterns and stages. We know that each child we teach is a unique creation of God, with special characteristics and personality traits. To be an effective teacher, it is important to personalize learning and build a relationship with each child. At the same time, it is

**HANDS ON**

**Think of a child you know. Using the areas and characteristics listed, describe that child.**

helpful to know something about children as a group. Most children ages 6-11 develop within these broad, general guidelines.

*Mentally*, children are:
Curious and continually learning
Able to make choices
Predominantly literal thinkers but beginning to grasp abstract concepts
Strengthening their language abilities
Creative and inventive in their ideas and plans
Able to focus on a task for longer periods of time
Becoming independent thinkers
Desiring an active role in group decision making

*Socially*, children are:
Able to work on group projects
Developing friendships with same-sex peers
Becoming able to demonstrate altruism and empathy
Showing an interest in other cultures and their needs
Understanding rules and consequences
Loyal to friends and teammates

*Emotionally*, children are:
Seeking affirmation of individual gifts and talents
Growing more independent
Aware of own strengths and limitations
Developing a sense of belonging
Expressing feelings openly
Anxious in large groups of unknown people
Judging self according to adult interactions
Realizing what triggers others' feelings, emotions, and needs

*Physically*, children are:
Active learners
Utilizing all their senses
Becoming more coordinated
Increasingly able to use fine motor skills
Experiencing uneven growth spurts
Enjoying more organized sports and board games

*Spiritually*, children are:

Developing a sense of right and wrong

Learning to pray

Developing the ability to participate actively in worship

Growing in their faith in God

Familiar with many Bible teachings

Relating knowledge of the Bible and Christian faith to daily life

Acquiring biblical knowledge, skills, and principles for making right choices

Learning to trust Christ without question

## Teaching Children with Special Needs

Jesus had a way of making everyone feel they belonged. From tax collectors to prostitutes, cripples to lepers, women to children, all people were included in the circle of Jesus' love and care. Jesus serves as our model for inclusion, the belief that all children—gifted, at-risk, physically, emotionally, and profoundly handicapped— are to be included in the group and have their needs appropriately met. Teachers often feel inadequate or fearful of inclusion, having been instilled with the perception

**Many teachers have come to enjoy the vision of all children working side by side at church, experiencing success, developing lifelong friendships, and fostering an attitude of acceptance.**

that they are not special education teachers and therefore cannot teach those with special education needs.

Children who are physically challenged, mentally challenged, or gifted may exhibit varying rates of development. Teachers can strive to meet each child's special needs through careful observation, a close working relationship with parents, and an understanding of the development and needs of the child. When possible, children with special needs should be grouped with those close to their own age. Other children of the same age may be the best support for children with disabilities.

## Mentally Delayed Children

Mentally delayed children learn and process information more slowly than their normally developing peers. Children with significant mental retardation experience difficulty with language development, memory, and attention. Generally, mentally delayed children require more time to produce a response and have trouble using skills in new situations.

To assist children with significant mental disabilities, the teacher can
• speak more slowly and increase the length of pauses.
• use repetition.
• create a predictable environment.
• give very specific directions one at a time
• vary the pace so children have time to concentrate as well as relax
• provide multisensory tasks

## Intellectually Gifted Children

Intellectually gifted children are advanced mentally and flourish in an atmosphere that provides challenge and an opportunity to expand creatively. Gifted children are curious; tend to pose interesting questions, think about problems and how to solve them, seek relationships and patterns, view learning as an adventure, and are

On occasion, additional teachers may be needed to provide individual assistance.

Broader definitions of giftedness now include exceptional abilities in the arts, leadership skills, spatial reasoning, and talent that utilizes body movement.

motivated to plan and implement projects. Such children may be particularly sensitive to the feelings of adults. They can be skillful manipulators and need help in using their special gifts, not abusing them.

To encourage gifted children, the teacher can:
- provide activities that enhance creativity
- encourage brain storming of ideas
- allow honest expression of emotion
- show interest in their thoughts and creative efforts
- be flexible, allowing extra time for open-ended projects

## Children who Lack Self-Control

Children who lack self-control are usually described as aggressive, hostile, impulsive, or hyperactive. Such children find it difficult to behave appropriately and follow the rules of conduct. Hostile and aggressive children may strike out deliberately, while hyperactive and impulsive children may often be unable to control their actions.

**Attention deficit children can be trying to teachers and parents, yet often are very bright and creative.**

More and more children are diagnosed each year with ADHD (Attention Deficit Hyperactivity Disorder), a problem that prevents them from focusing attention on a task and completing it. Some ADHD children are physically jumpy, uncontrolled, impulsive, and very active; others are irresponsible, disorganized, and dreamy.

To help children with attention deficits, the teacher can:
- be patient
- tolerate a higher level of activity than normal.
- prevent over-stimulation by limiting noise level and visual images
- provide quiet places
- serve as models for patience, problem solving, and organization
- reward good behavior, not bad, with attention
- help children set realistic goals

## Children with Physical Disabilities

Children with physical disabilities may need special classroom accommodations, but are as mentally developed as other children their age. Physical impairments may include hearing loss, visual problems, and disabling conditions that require wheelchair usage.

**Children with Hearing Loss**

To assist a child with hearing loss, the teacher can:
- ask parents to teach her the signs they use
- be sure that windows or other light sources are not behind her or shining into the eyes of the child
- speak slowly, using gestures, facial expressions, and pictures
- stand or sit still while talking
- check the sound level of different areas of the room to accommodate a child with a hearing aid

**Children with Limited Vision**

To support a child with limited vision, the teacher can:
- avoid "bombarding" the child with too much talk
- touch the child to convey that you are listening
- be sure the child uses vision as much as possible
- talk about what you are doing and what the child is doing as it happens
- keep furniture in the same spot
- help the child see and feel all parts of an object and understand the relationship of parts to a whole

To include a child with physical disabilities, the teacher can

- involve the child in movement activities as much as possible without highlighting the inability to move well
- measure assistive devices such as wheelchairs, and walkers to ensure adequate movement and space within the room, through doorways, and under tables
- teach all children how to safely operate a wheelchair for another child
- vary activities in a group with activities alone or with a partner

## The Environment for Special Needs Children

Take time to look at your room and see how it is arranged so that special needs children can experience

**HANDS ON**

**Using the characteristics listed, describe a child you know with special needs.**

success. Think ahead and plan ways to enable children with disabilities to meet the following special challenges:

**Visual Challenges:** Create learning centers with clearly defined borders to help make the classroom more accessible. Provide learning activities recorded on audio tape. Add items of various textures to each area so multisensory learning experiences are provided.

**Hearing Challenges:** Plan activities and materials that hearing impaired children can manage independently. Place simple drawings and symbols in the room to remind them of simple rules and procedures. Write instructions for learning activities on cards.

**Physical Challenges:** Arrange learning areas for comfort and support with materials at children's eye level. Provide carpet with a nonskid backing and choose heavy, sturdy furniture that will hold the weight of a child. Make sure a child in a wheelchair has easy access to shelves, supplies, and tables. Use several activities designed for children to do by themselves.

**Mental Challenges:** Design activities that meet a wide range of developmental stages. Use clear and consistent cues to designate different areas, such as the use of color. Look for more ways to develop learning centers and games that provide repetition. Present new information and materials in manageable portions so that children can experience success.

**Social/Emotional Challenges:** Consider making some aspects of your environment less stimulating, especially if children seem to be over-stimulated or confused. Children need quiet spots to be alone. Limit some choices and vary the length of time for activities. Provide time in the schedule for one-on-one time with children who need extra support.

The ministry/learning environment should reflect the diversity of children and their differing abilities. All children, those with special needs along with those who do not require special accommodation, need to see themselves reflected in the world around them. Books, images, learning materials, and role models should be available depicting children and adults with disabilities engaged in a variety of activities. Children with disabilities need both acceptance for who they are and an environment that supports their independence and alternative means of interaction with the world.

**Now describe how you could change the room environment in which you teach to adapt to the needs of that child.**

Listen to my instruction and be wise; do not ignore it. Proverbs 8:33

# Chapter 3
# Children and Learning

## By Chris Ward

Mr. Anderson is leading the first-graders in a study of the story of creation. The children are sitting with him on the floor examining shells, pods, bones, goldfish, snakeskin, rocks, and a bird's nest. A lively discussion takes place as Mr. Anderson asks, "Why do you think God created light and dark before He created the animals?"

In Mrs. Juarez' choir room the children are excited as they prepare a basket of fruit for Mrs. Watson, a diabetic who no longer attends church. As Mrs. Juarez plays the Autoharp, the children sing the hymns they plan to share with Mrs. Watson. A book filled with pictures and messages from each child is ready. "When we get to her house, can we all pray together?" asks Molly.

Mr. Reynolds brings a snack to Children's Bible Drill in order to have time to visit with each child. The children form Study-Buddy pairs and practice reviewing key Bible verses and locating books of the Bible. Mr. Reynolds walks around the room, encouraging them and giving assistance when needed. Then the entire group participates in a mock Bible drill, discussing the areas of success and where they need to improve.

Each of these teachers understands the different ways children learn because teachers are responsible for helping children learn in the most effective way possible. At church, children are learning continuously about God and His plan for their lives. Because this is such an important ministry, teachers need to have a deeper understanding of how children think and learn.

*Children learn by using prior knowledge to actively engage them in personally meaningful tasks.* They learn by doing and by thinking about what they are doing. By building upon what they already know, children make mental connections.

The boys and girls you teach at church come knowing something about God. Some children have prior church experience even before you met them as well as parents who see the home as the center of biblical guidance. Others come with misconceptions about God based on exposure to ideas reflected in the media. Regardless of varying experiences, when children are immersed in Bible teachings that apply to their lives, they are more likely to realize daily their personal need for God .

While we know children learn by doing, it is also true that mere manipulation of objects does not ensure mental engagement. Just because Amanda completes the jigsaw puzzle of Jesus' resurrection does not mean she understands the spiritual significance of the event. Likewise, children may leave Sunday School having had fun painting and drawing, but with no understanding of how the activities connect to God's plan for their lives.

*Children learn when adults guide them towards an understanding of Bible truths as the children are ready.* For learning to occur, adults must know each child personally. Knowing each child's unique abilities and understanding typical expectations for children in the group provide a more complete foundation for determining readiness.

**Which statements about learning do you think most affects learning at church?**

**Write your reasons in the margin beside each of those statements.**

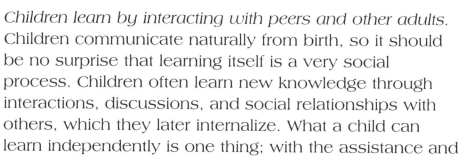

*Children learn by interacting with peers and other adults.* Children communicate naturally from birth, so it should be no surprise that learning itself is a very social process. Children often learn new knowledge through interactions, discussions, and social relationships with others, which they later internalize. What a child can learn independently is one thing; with the assistance and encouragement of a strong teacher or more capable peers, the potential for learning is increased. Sharing ideas with one another fosters higher level thinking skills and improves the collective understanding of God and biblical truths.

*Children learn best from caring adults with whom they have personal relationships.* If our goal as teachers is to lead children in developing a personal relationship with Jesus Christ, it follows that our relationship with each child will serve as a model. Children will seek to understand the abstract quality of God and His love through the people who share with them that love and care. As models children will follow, teachers must recognize the importance of a covenant relationship with Jesus. When teachers are living their lives for Christ, it is apparent in their actions and behavior, and the children notice.

*Learning experiences are most valuable when based on the variety of ways children learn and share knowledge.* Children are individuals created by God and are equiped to learn in many ways. Because learning is developmental and individual, children do not learn at the same rate nor have the same interest in learning. Each learner has a preferred learning style that is the best way or the most natural means of learning. Some children prefer listening, while others learn best through seeing or moving.

Children utilize several types of intelligences as they construct knowledge, which provides multiple ways of learning concepts, skills, and ideas. Similarly, children demonstrate what they know in different ways. When teachers consider children's multiple ways of learning, it means children at any age can approach a Bible story or truth from a variety of meaningful learning perspectives.

*Learning that is real involves authentic performance— doing something real.* When children have a vital interest in the learning experience, they are most likely to learn from it. Quality learning occurs when a child is involved in an experience that is authentic. For example, Mrs.

Juarez' choir does not practice hymns and songs just as an exercise in recognizing notes; a broader purpose more important than the musical knowledge is gained. Mrs. Juarez is encouraging the children to do something real—to learn Bible truths and to share their talents, time, and care with a shut-in. Doing something real is being like Jesus and sharing God's love with others.

*Children make sense of their learning by applying it to other situations.* Being able to transfer knowledge, ideas, and concepts from one setting to another is an essential part of learning. Children need to hear Bible stories, verses, and truths repeatedly before they can become an integral part of their lives. The repetition aids in the learning process and provides a foundational knowledge and understanding. Then the child is ready to seek ways to apply biblical truths at home, at school, at church, and in the community.

*Children also must practice what they learn.* A teacher who expects the children to report back to the group as to how the task was accomplished instills commitment. "Last Sunday we made a pledge to do what our Bible verse said. Will one of you tell us what you did this week that showed kindness to another person?"

## Kinds of Learning

Typically, learning is described in three broad categories—*cognitive learning, affective learning,* and *psychomotor learning.* Each of these types of learning is of equal importance in meeting the needs of the whole child. However, our schools tend to value cognitive achievement more than other areas. As we lead children to know God, to love Him completely, and to follow His commands, each area of learning must be encouraged and strengthened.

*Cognitive learning* involves knowledge and the act of knowing. This area of learning focuses on the thinking process and knowledge itself. When planning for the

cognitive domain, we might ask, "What is important for the child to know? What is important for the child to understand?" Cognitive learning would include knowledge of Bible stories, meaning of terms, memory verses, and biblical truths. We encourage cognitive growth when we work with children to build understanding of complex concepts, compare and contrast key ideas, analyze events, and draw conclusions.

*Affective learning* focuses on attitudes and emotions. How you feel about what you are learning is an integral part of the learning process. For example, if you lack confidence in your mathematical ability and have a bad attitude toward math, your feelings will begin to impact your performance. When planning for the affective domain, we might ask, "How does the child feel about this? How can we help the child express how she feels about this?" Teachers can lead children to discover their emotional response to a Bible story by having them consider how they would feel in the place of the person being studied. We support affective learning when we help children grow in self-awareness and self-esteem, develop empathy for others' feelings, and model ways to handle emotions.

*Psychomotor learning* is the mental activity that results in body movement involving both small and large muscles. It is the area of learning concerned with doing, moving, and manipulating. When planning for the psychomotor domain, we might ask, "As a result of this, what can the child do? What motor skills are being developed?" Children acquire psychomotor learning as they make maps, sing hymns, plant seeds, create art, dramatize a Bible story, use puppets, and play instruments. We convey the importance of psychomotor learning when we build gross and fine motor skills, foster care and respect for the body, and promote healthy attitudes toward physical activity.

One teacher has her fifth graders do a reflective exercise after each Bible study that addresses the three types of learning. Each child completes an index card by
- drawing a head (cognitive) and completing this sentence:
  The most important thing I learned today is...
- drawing a heart (affective) and completing this sentence:
  What I learned today made me feel...
- drawing a foot (psychomotor) and completing this sentence: As a result of what I learned today, I plan to...

**Look at a session in your leader guide. Determine which activities fall into the categories of cognitive learning, affective learning, and psychomotor learning. Place a C beside the activities that reflect cognitive learning, an A beside the activities that reflect affective learning, and a P beside the activities that reflect psychomotor learning.**

## What the Latest Brain Research Tells Us

New research in medical and cognitive sciences is increasing our knowledge about how the brain works. These findings provide new ways of thinking about how children learn and develop.

Three key findings of recent brain research are:
- A child's capacity to learn and "bloom" in a variety of settings depends on the interaction of nature (the unique way God created him) and nurture (the kind of care and teaching he receives).
- The human brain is uniquely constructed to benefit from experience and good teaching, particularly during the first ten years of life.
- While learning continues throughout life, there are times when the brain is best at certain types of learning. Until about age 12, the brain masters more easily such tasks as speaking a new language or learning to play a musical instrument, tasks that are much more difficult for adolescents and adults.

What do these findings mean to those who teach children? First, all children can learn. Second, good teaching is the key to learning. Research demonstrates repeatedly that as children's senses are stimulated by experiences that ask them to see, hear, taste, and move, brain networks are strengthened. Teachers who encourage hands-on learning, questions, and interactions with other children are working to build better brains! Finally, children ages 6-11 are in an optimum stage for learning and can be exposed to many new concepts and ideas. Repetition, practice, and an opportunity to discuss questions help children make sense of new knowledge.

## Learning Styles and Multiple Intelligences

Children are learning continuously and each child approaches learning in a unique manner. Some children prefer to read Bible stories about Joseph, others would rather hear the teacher tell the story, and still others want to create Joseph's coat of many colors and act out the story. While children learn in a variety of ways, most children have a preferred learning style that involves seeing, hearing, or doing.

*Visual learners* like to see things as they learn. They enjoy reading, making maps, designing charts and graphs, using the computer, writing, creating posters, and working puzzles. Visual learners are good at seeing ideas in their minds and visualizing what they are hearing. A room rich in maps, Bible verses, labels, picture, and books, is beneficial to the visual learner.

*Auditory learners* like to hear as they learn. They enjoy listening to audio-tapes, hearing Bible stories, retelling stories in their own words, singing, reciting poetry, and talking with other people. Auditory learners usually like word games and discussions, but dislike reading silently. *Kinesthetic learners* like to move as they learn. They prefer moving around and using their bodies. Kinesthetic learners choose activities such as acting out Bible stories, playing games, pantomime, and playing

instruments. They like to build dioramas or models and handle objects. Kinesthetic learners use gestures and body language to communicate and need many opportunities to move out of their chairs to engage in purposeful activity.

Children develop and practice a mix of styles as they grow and learn. Most people practice all three styles to varying degrees. Teachers should help each child discover her unique preferences for learning.

# Multiple Intelligences

In addition to learning styles, children come with many God-given intelligences (not just IQ!). Here are eight intelligences that you may see in the children you teach. Many children are strong in more than one intelligence, but all possess varying abilities in most areas.

| Intelligence | Description | Applications |
|---|---|---|
| Verbal | Uses language to express ideas and understand others | writing in a journal reading the Bible listening to a story telling about an experience |
| Logical | Uses reasoning Uses logical problem solving Thinks mathematically | making projects following a plan looking for patterns solving brain teasers |
| Visual | Forms images of the world in the mind | expressing ideas without words (drawing, photos, making posters) playing board games building models |
| Physical | Uses his body to make something or solve a problem | using movement enacting a play pantomime helping a sick friend engaging in active games |
| Musical | Is sensitive to music, rhythm, and beat | creating raps and songs playing instruments humming, whistling appreciating different kinds of music learning songs about people in the Bible |

| Intelligence | Description | Applications |
| --- | --- | --- |
| Interpersonal | gets along and works well with others | working with others on projects<br>cooperative group learning<br>discussing problems |
| Intrapersonal | Knows who she is and what she can and cannot do | keeping a journal<br>writing about self<br>choosing to do a task alone<br>sharing a special hobby |
| Naturalist | Sensitive to God's creation and has an ability to identify things in nature | caring for plants and pets<br>taking nature walks<br>making collections of natural materials such as leaves and rocks |

**HANDS ON**

Determine which of the eight intelligences is your dominant intelligence.

Explain why you think so.

## The Ministry/Learning Environment

In planning the learning environment, it is important to consider both emotional and physical factors. Both areas influence how children develop, behave, and learn. Planning an emotional environment means creating a caring community that supports warm, comfortable relationships between teachers, children, and their families. Children are excited about coming and participating in learning activities because they feel they belong to the group.

*Children feel cared for and loved.* When children come into the room, teachers who are prepared and planned greet them. Children feel accepted and included and can find a place to be successful in the room. Adults take time to listen to each child and build relationships. A positive climate for learning is a setting that encourages children to share their ideas, to respect themselves and others, and to show by their actions that they love others.

*Children are offered choices and opportunities to take risks.* When children feel secure in their environment, they will take more risks as they learn. Whether it is praying aloud or choosing a center that seems more challenging, children are more willing to try new things and learn from mistakes when they choose activities of interest to them.

*Children's families are included and kept informed.* Newsletters, phone calls, home visits, and email messages are all examples of ways to communicate with families as our partners in the work of the church. Parents should feel welcome to drop in and see what is happening in the rooms where their children are taught.

*Children feel ownership for what happens in the room.* The room belongs to the children and should reflect some of their choices in how to share what they are learning about God. When children have a part in developing the department rules, they will be more likely to act upon those rules.

*Children treat one another with respect and kindness as they work together.* When adults respect children and empathize with their feelings, children learn what respect looks like. Children feel important when teachers show delight in them by smiling, laughing, and paying attention to what they say.

**Space Requirements for Children, Grades 1-6**
- **25 sq. ft. per person**
- **maximum group size: 30**
- **room size: 750 sq. ft.**

The physical environment is as important as the emotional environment because the way the room looks, smells, and feels tells visitors a lot about the teaching and learning occurring there. Features of the physical environment include space, time, materials, and mood.

- Space—Children need space to move and participate in activities. The way space is utilized has a direct impact on behavior and learning. Teachers usually try to arrange space into areas for whole group activities, small group activities, and quiet spots for independent work. Twenty-five square feet per person is recommended for children's teaching rooms.

- Time—Use time flexibly. Children need blocks of time for active exploration and deeper understanding of Bible truths. Alternating active times with more structured large group instruction will help keep more children engaged in learning.

- Materials—An environment that supports children's learning contains appropriate learning materials that interest children and meet their individual needs. To promote learning, materials should be accessible to children, labeled, well organized, and stored neatly on shelves. All children are responsible for the care and cleanup of materials.

- Mood—Our senses help bring the atmosphere or feel of the classroom to life. A room with natural light is inviting and cheerful to learners. Color also contributes to the feeling of an environment, but should not overwhelm the senses. Soft pastel colors such as pale green, blue, and yellow work well on walls. Carpet adds texture, reduces noise, and provides a comfortable place to work. Good ventilation and a comfortable room temperature add to a positive mood.

Love one another. As I have loved you. So you must love one another. By this shall all men know that you are my disciples, if you love one another. John 13:34-35

# Chapter 4
# Children Learn from Their Leaders

## By Anne Tonks

Mrs. Morrison stood at the door to the third-grade Sunday School room. She watched Kyle and Jason work on a Bible-verse mobile, "A friend loves at all times" (Prov. 17:17). She listened as the boys talked together.

"Boy, that's a hard thing to do," Kyle commented.

Cutting out the triangles?" asked Jason with a puzzled look on his face.

"No," Kyle answered. "Loving other people all the time. Sometimes I just hate my sister. She can be so mean."

"Yeah," Jason agreed. "I don't know anybody who loves everybody all the time!"

Mrs. Morrison smiled as she approached the boys. She admired the work they were doing on the mobile.

"You're right," she said to the boys. "I don't know any-body nowadays like that either. But Jesus was. And God wants us to try as hard as we can to be like Jesus. He even promised us that He would help us. Let's all try really hard and we can even remind each other of how God wants us to live."

"You know what?" Jason said to Kyle. "I bet Mrs. Morrison loves everybody all the time. I know she loves us."

**Think of the teacher who had the most significant influence on your life. Write a letter to that teacher, telling her several things you remember about how she lived. Help her know how much she helped you live the life God wants you to live.**

**Dear                  ,**

Mrs. Morrison knew that a significant way in which children learn is by watching and copying or modeling what the grownups around them do and say. She knew that whenever she told a Bible story, helped a child learn a memory verse, or talked about God and Jesus, the children were watching her behavior as much or more as they were listening to her words. She knew that if she did not follow the teachings of Jesus in her own life that the children would observe that and ignore the words she said, no matter how true those words were.

Mrs. Morrison also knew that as she taught the children how to pray, that she must spend time in prayer. She knew that as she helped them memorize Bible verses, she must learn the verses too. She knew that as she helped the children know how to have a daily quiet time with God, that she must develop the same habit. She knew that as she taught them how to live as Jesus lived, she must do the same.

## Jesus as Our Model

As Jesus taught people how God wanted them to live, He modeled for them the very life He was describing. He provided bread and fish when people had nothing to eat. He was kind to the children when the disciples would have sent them away. He became a friend to Zacchaeus when others shunned him. Jesus supported Mary when Judas denounced her for pouring expensive perfume on His feet. Jesus even asked God to forgive those responsible for His death!

**In His name,**

*Principle of Biblical Leadership*
**Sunday School calls leaders to follow the biblical standard of leadership.**

One of the five principles of Sunday School is the *Principle of Biblical Leadership*. The principle states that "Sunday School calls leaders to follow the biblical standard of leadership." That sounds simple and logical, doesn't it? Live as Jesus lived. His example is in the Scriptures for us to read and follow. But how easy is it?

**HANDS ON**

1. Emily has just started to come to your church. Her family does not come. She is in the fourth grade but has repeated one year at school. She is older than the other children and always seems to be angry about something. She does not work well with the other fourth graders. They do not seem to like her. You don't like her very much either. Teaching the group has become a chore for you. *What would Jesus do?* List some things you could do to improve the situation.

In the space following each situation, write what you think would be some ways in which Jesus would behave in these situations.

2. Jackson regularly attends every group offered for children at the church. He is well-liked by the other children because he has an amusing personality and is fun to be around. Unfortunately he does not always settle down and his behavior distracts the other girls and boys. He is bright, he knows all the answers, and he finishes his assignments quickly; so he has extra time on his hands. You like Jackson but realize that he often controls the group. You don't want to discourage him, but you also know that the children are not learning as much as they should. *What would Jesus do?* List several things you will do to help Jackson as well as the other girls and boys.

## Jesus Modeled Love

While Jesus was on earth, He showed us the ways in which God wants people to live. He modeled love, kindness, concern, and compassion. He told others about God. He spent time alone with God. He went to God for guidance and support. How can we do less? Pray that God will give you the strength you need to live like Jesus and model His ways for the girls and boys you teach.

When Jesus was asked what was the greatest commandment, He answered, "'Love the Lord your God with all your heart and with all your soul and with all your mind.' This is the first and greatest commandment. And the second is like it: 'Love your neighbor as yourself'" (Matt. 22:37-39). Jesus understood the full meaning of loving others. Not only did He consistently demonstrate a loving, caring attitude toward His disciples and the people who came to hear Him teach; He demonstrated the same attitude toward those who hated Him.

As Jesus taught about God, he modeled love because God *is* love. Moses knew that. He and the Israelite people sang to God, "In your unfailing love you will lead the people you have redeemed (Ex. 15:13). David knew it, too. Many times throughout the Psalms he spoke of God's "unfailing love" And Paul knew it. He wrote these words to the church at Rome, "For I am convinced that neither death nor life, neither angels nor demons, neither the present nor the future, nor any powers, neither height nor depth, nor anything else in all creation, will be able to separate us from the love of God that is in Christ Jesus our Lord (Rom. 8:38-39). And he wrote an entire chapter on love to the people in the church at Corinth.

Angela loved children. When she was a little girl she used to play school with her friends. She was always the teacher. When she became a teenager she began to babysit for some of the families in her neighborhood. As a youth, she went on mission trips and taught Vacation Bible School. Then as a college student she began to teach girls and boys in Sunday School.

**HANDS ON**

The children Angela taught knew she loved them because she smiled at them as they entered the room. She listened as they told her about things happening in their lives. She was patient with them as they worked on their projects or learned a memory verse. Angela visited the children in their homes, planned get-togethers, and showed concern when a child hesitantly told her about a problem. She laughed with the children as they played games. Angela understood what modeling God's love meant. And Angela also knew that the children were learning from her behavior. So she tried to live her life as God would have her live.

Showing love to the children we teach, however, is not only being kind, patient and understanding. Loving children is also being aware of what they need to learn and what is appropriate behavior for them to display. As Jesus dealt with the crowds of people, He often posed questions that were difficult to answer or gave directives

50

that were not easy to follow. He never left the impression that following in God's ways would be easy.

One day a rich young man asked Jesus how he could have eternal life. When Jesus told him to live a good life, the young man answered that he already kept all the commandments. Then Jesus told him to give away his possessions to the poor. Those words were not what the young man wanted to hear and so he "went away sad, because he had great wealth" (Matt. 19:22).

On another occasion, Jesus reprimanded His disciples for sending some parents and children away. In fact, Jesus was indignant (Matt. 10:14). He said to the disciples, "I tell you the truth, anyone who will not receive the kingdom of God like a little child will never inherit it" (Matt. 10:15).

In His wisdom, Jesus knew when He needed to do or say things that would help people in their search for God and His will for their lives. A teacher of girls and boys also needs to be aware of when and how to guide the children in appropriate ways.

## Jesus Modeled Obedience

*And whatever you do, whether in word or deed, do it all in the name of the Lord Jesus, giving thanks to God the Father through him.* Colossians 3:17

When Jesus came to earth, not only was He to tell the people about God; but He had before Him a very difficult responsibility. Jesus had to face His own death by crucifixion. Yet knowing that did not change His mind. God wanted Jesus to live on earth and Jesus obeyed Him. When the time came for Jesus to be crucified, He prayed, "Father, if you are willing, take this cup from me; yet not my will, but yours be done" (Luke 22:42). What an amazing model for obedience!

The Bible gives many examples of obedience. God told Noah to build an ark to save his family and the animals, and Noah obeyed God. He paid no attention to the fact

**Are there children who are not quite as easy to love? Write their names here.**

**Now choose one name from each group. Think of how each child lives his life. List several ways in which you will relate to each child that will help him know how God wants him to live.**

that there wasn't any water nearby. He simply did what God told him to do. When God gave Abraham and Sarah a son in their old age, they were overjoyed. But when God told Abraham to take Isaac and sacrifice him, Abraham obeyed. The Bible does not tell us how Abraham may have felt or what his thoughts were as he and Isaac went to the place of sacrifice; but he did not waver. When Isaac asked where the sacrifice was, Abraham said, "God himself will provide the lamb for the burnt offering' (Gen. 22:8).

Mr. Jackson taught preteens in his church. He enjoyed being with the age group. The preteens liked Mr. Jackson, too. They also respected him. They knew that when he told them something about God that he really believed it. The preteens watched as Mr. Jackson sat in church with his wife and two children, five and six years old. They noticed that he was kind to the children. They watched as he helped the children find hymns in the hymnbook. They noticed how he always answered their questions. So one day when Mr. Jackson had to talk to the preteens on a serious topic, they listened. They knew that Mr. Jackson obeyed God and he wanted to help them learn to obey God, too.

## Jesus Modeled Self Discipline

*Let us be self-controlled, putting on faith and love as a breastplate, and the hope of salvation as a helmet.* 1 Thessalonians 5:8

Jesus was very aware of His purpose here on earth. He knew what He had to do and He did it. When Jesus saw people who needed His help, He helped them. When He was weary, He rested. When He needed to spend time with God, He withdrew by Himself. He taught the crowds who came to hear Him tell about God until He was exhausted. But He kept that one purpose in His mind. He used His time wisely because He knew the time he had to accomplish His task was limited.

For additional help in disciplining your personal life, see the "Life Helps" section of the *Disciples Study Bible.*

**HANDS ON**

As a teacher, your time is probably limited, too. That is why it is important to see clearly the task to which God has called you–helping children learn about Him, His ways, and His plan for their lives. Look over the suggestions below and mark at least three in each category that you will implement immediately.

Discipline yourself in your personal life:

_____ Plan a specific time to spend with God every day.

_____ Choose some devotional books that will help you focus on God.

_____ Start a prayer journal.

_____ Form a group of close Christian friends who will be your prayer partners.

Discipline yourself to learn about children.

_____ Study a book on how children develop.

_____ Study information on how children learn.

_____ Ask your children about the kinds of things they like to do outside of Sunday School.

_____ Visit the children to see the homes they live in.

**The children you teach are watching you. Do they see in you an adult who leads a transformed life?**

As you teach your girls and boys, remember that you are trying to help them develop self-control and self-discipline too. You are helping them know what it means to live in God's ways. But you and the other adults in each child's life will not always be around. So the child must be taught not only the words of God's commandments, but what those words mean. Children need help determining the specific actions they will take as they live godly lives. Don't assume that children automatically know the ways in which God wants them to live. A good, loving teacher will comment on a child when she observes behavior that is pleasing to God.

"Jenny, I like the way you helped Kathy finish her Bible-learning activity. God likes us to help others, doesn't he?"

"Jonathan, thank you for being a friend to Jack today. The Bible tells us to be kind to others. You did just what God would want you to do."

# Qualities of a Good Teacher

Remember the teacher you wrote about earlier in this chapter? Think of her again. Think of some of the qualities that teacher possessed. Chances are, you will find most of those qualities in this word search. Find and circle as many as you can find. The words go from left to right and from top to bottom and all are located in the box below.

```
C H R I S T I A N A P A B
A D E P E N D A B L E C D
L G X A L E F G H I A J K
L O A T F L M N O P C Q R
E O M I – S T U V W E X Y
D D P E C F K Z A B F C G
D E L N O G I H I J U K E
L M E T N O N P Q R L S N
T U V S T U D I O U S W T
X Y Z J R A B C D E F G L
H I C O O P E R A T I V E
J K L Y L O V I N G R S T
U V W F L X Y Z A B C D E
F G H U E I J K L M N O P
Q R S L D T U V W X Y Z A
```

Trust in the Lord with all your heart and lean not on your own understanding; in all your ways acknowledge him, and he will make your paths straight.
Proverbs 3:5-6

# Chapter 5
# A Purpose for Teaching
## By David Morrow

One summer I worked with the contractor who built our new church. He used several guys who needed summer money and he saved himself a bundle on skilled labor. The first thing we did was dig the holes for the footings, the foundation. The contractor liked to save money, so rather than bringing in a backhoe, he gave us shovels. What a job that was! And more than twenty-five years later the church still stands. Those deep holes filled with steel rods and concrete became the foundation for a building that will last for years.

### The Principles of Sunday School

*Sunday School is the foundational strategy in a local church for leading people to faith in the Lord Jesus Christ and for building Great Commission Christians through Bible study groups that engage people in evangelism, discipleship, fellowship, ministry, and worship.*

**Write here your purpose in teaching boys and girls in Sunday School.**

**Pray and seek God's direction as you reflect on what you are doing and why.**

Jesus tells of the importance of building on the right foundation (Matt. 7:24-27). The Sunday School that soon began to meet in that building needed a foundation, too. In fact, the whole strategy of Sunday School is built on five principles. These principles become the foundation for Sunday School. In other words the success or failure of the Sunday School is dependent on getting these five principles right, just as that church building was dependent on me digging those deep holes. The five principles are:

- The Principle of Foundational Evangelism
- The Principle of Foundational Discipleship
- The Principle of Family Responsibility
- The Principle of Spiritual Transformation
- The Principle of Biblical Leadership

## The Principle of Foundational Evangelism

You've been picked!

I can well remember those sandlot baseball or football games. It seems that I was always the shortest in the crowd and often the last chosen for a team. But I was just glad to be a player. As the game went on I played extra hard to prove myself in preparation for the next draft. I loved to play.

As a children's Sunday School leader you have been picked for another team. Statistics tell us that even though only about 14% of our Sunday School enrollment is in grades one through six, over 30% of the reported baptisms comes from those same six years. In the same vein, a study done by the Barna Research Institute pointed out that before age 12 there is a 32% likelihood of becoming a Christian. However only a four percent chance a person will become a Christian between 12 and 18 and a six percent likelihood an individual will become a Christian after 18[1].

Those statistics underline the crucial nature of these six years. From the foundations of the early years to the realization of the reality of sin, guided Bible study (Sunday School) makes a great difference. Children's Sunday

School workers will have the opportunity to share their faith with parents as well as children who have reached a point of conviction for sin. I am convinced that there is no greater joy in heaven or earth than when someone accepts Jesus as their Savior.

Think about these questions. Do you know the spiritual condition of the children, parents, and families in your department? Have you read about Care4Kids or Contact 1•2•3 in your Sunday School leader's guide? Has your pastor considered attending a FAITH clinic so that your church can be a part of an intentional evangelism strategy? Would you consider being a part of a FAITH team in your church?

## The Principle of Foundational Discipleship

Just like Papa! One of the joys of my life is my grandson Coleman David. Coleman is only 18 months old, but already people tell me, "He looks just like you!" As a grandpa, there is nothing more exciting than to see another generation come along that reflects some of my characteristics. I usually tell those who compliment me about my grandson's good looks, "Just wait till his mustache comes in a little thicker and he will really look like Papa. "I guess as he grows older we will watch to see if he begins to act like family members as well as look like us.

That is Jesus' plan for His followers, His disciples. He planned for them to be like Him. Now I am convinced that the more time I spend with Coleman, the more like me he will become. The same is true of disciples. The only way to become more like Christ is to spend time with Him. Children spend time with Jesus in Sunday School through the Bible study and worship, Bible learning activities and relationships with teachers. In other words Sunday School provides foundational discipleship. It is the beginning point for understanding the Christian walk for most of us.

## The Principle of Family Responsibility

I just love the children in my Sunday School department. It is almost as if I have adopted each of those little third graders. I have a great responsibility for their well being and growth. I take that responsibility very seriously. but with all of the things that I can do as a teacher, the best thing that can happen for the children is for their families to accept the responsibility for the biblical guidance of their children.

Mom's, Dad's, adopted families, extended families, any combination that you can come up with, have a far greater influence on the future of my young third graders than I will ever have. What works best as a partnership is one where I as Sunday School teacher begin a study with their during the Bible-study time. Then throughout the week the family reviews, reinforces, and models the message of the study.

I can help families through notes and newsletters, Home pages and phone calls; but nothing can replace the dramatic influence of a parent who teaches daily at home. The results will last a lifetime ... no, an eternity. It's a small investment for such a *large* return.

## The Principle of Spiritual Transformation

Spiritual transformation is God's work of changing a believer into the likeness of Jesus by creating a new identity in Christ and by empowering a lifelong relationship of love, trust, and obedience to glorify God.

People never stop changing. From birth till death, each day brings about more change. The most significant of all changes is that of spiritual transformation. The focus of our Bible teaching is to help children grow in their understanding of God's message. As leaders in children's Sunday School, we are the pipelines for God's message. We help children learn and understand the truths of scripture through Bible study each week. The Holy Spirit then uses the learning and understanding to bring about spiritual transformation in the life of the child.

Two questions to ask about a children's Sunday School class or department are:
1. Has each leader had that personal experience of spiritual transformation? Is Romans 12:2 a reality of life? We need to make sure the pipeline is not clogged.
2. Is each Bible study focused on helping children see that God can change their lives?

The significance of prayer in the process cannot be underestimated. Look for ways to involve your entire church in prayer for the children. Ask adult classes to pray for the children each Sunday as they begin their class. Ask the children's teachers to walk down the halls or go to a children's room and pray for the boys and girls that will be in those rooms on Wednesday night. During your leadership meetings, pray for each child. Change comes about every day, but spiritual transformation needs your focus and intentional actions.

## The Principle of Biblical Leadership

I have heard it said for years, "The difference in churches is leadership." I did a quick look through an Internet search engine for the word *leadership*, then the word *crisis*, and then the combined words in the term *leadership crisis*. Over two and a half million pages are found that pick up on both leadership and crisis!

## My Challenge

We live in a world starving for great leaders in all walks of life. Work, school, sports, home, and church, all looking for leaders. Providing the right leaders for our children is a great concern. In some churches it really is a leadership crisis (disaster, catastrophe, emergency, calamity, predicament). So what can we do? We can follow a biblical model for leadership.

1. Pray to identify potential leaders.
2. Enlist the right leaders right away.
3. Determine the roles and responsibilities of the leadership team.

**Think of five persons you know in your church who would make good children's workers but are presently not working anywhere. Pray that God will speak to these persons about teaching children at church.**

1.Barna Research Online, www.barna.org/cgi-bin/PageCategory.asp?CategoryID=18

# Levels of Learning

The Levels of Learning[2] document is organized under three headings–God, self, and others–and offers teachers, parents, and leaders an approach for religious education that is biblically based and educationally appropriate. Under those headings, the document outlines the doctrinal teachings appropriate for preschoolers, children, and youth to study. That information is presented here. The appropriate biblical worldview categories appear in italics following each statement. Some basic assumptions related to levels of learning are as follows.

- The Bible is the basis for everything we teach children in Bible-study settings. All the content is based on Bible passages, Bible verses, and biblical principles.
- The Great Commission is at the center of teaching the Bible. The focus of our teaching is based on the five functions of evangelism, discipleship, ministry, fellowship, and worship. The end results are numerical growth, spiritual growth, ministries expansion, and missions advance. (1-5-4 Principle)
- Preschooler, children, and youth are the focus of our teaching.

The Levels of Learning document offers these benefits.

- Provides curriculum builders with an integrated, focused plan detailing accomplishment levels designated for certain ages or grade levels (found in the larger document).
- Gives a coordinated approach from birth through eighteen by using the same content areas.
- Deals with the transition in information and methodology between the older preschooler and younger children's area, the transition from children to youth and from youth to young adult.

## God, the Father

Doctrinal Teachings

1. God is the one true God. He is eternal, with no beginning and no end. He is unchanging and dependable. (Deut. 6:4; Isa. 44:6; 45:22; Heb. 13:8; Jas. 1:17) *Faith and Reason; Time and Eternity; God;*

2. God is all-loving, all-powerful, all-knowing, omnipresent, and infinitely holy. (Lev. 19:1-2; Job 36:22; Pss. 25:10; 139:1-13; 148:13; Isa. 6:1-3; Lam. 3:22-23; Luke 12:6-7; 1 John 4:8) *God; Creation, Sovereignty and Providence; Covenant and Redemption;*

3. God created the heavens and the earth and set in motion a plan to sustain His creation. God is at work in the world today. (Gen. 1–2; Job 38–39; Ps. 90:1-2; 104; Isa. 14:24, 26-27; Phil. 1:6; 2:13; Rev. 4:11) *God; Time and Eternity; Sovereignty and Providence; Creation*

4. Because of God's great love and mercy, He has provided a way for all people to know Him personally through Jesus (John 3:16; Rom. 5:8; 8:32; 2 Pet. 3:9; 1 John 4:9-10) *God; Covenant and Redemption; Revelation and Authority*

5. God is Heavenly Father, worthy of our highest love, reverence, worship, trust, and obedience. (1 Chron. 16:25; Pss. 5:7; 56:4; Isa. 6:1-3; Matt. 22:37; John 15:10; Rev. 4:11) *God; Revelation and Authority*

## God: Jesus, God's Son

Doctrinal Teachings

1. Jesus' life reveals that the eternal Son of God came to earth fully human while remaining fully divine, identifying Himself with sinners while remaining sinless. (Luke 2; 4:1-13; John 4:4-8; Heb. 2:18; 4:15) *Covenant and Redemption; Humanity; Revelation and Authority; God*

2. Jesus' virgin birth, miracles, authoritative teaching, and resurrection reveal that He was fully divine while remaining fully human, the Messiah sent by God. (Isa. 7:14; Matt. 14:13-21; Mark 10:46-52; Luke 4:14-21; 15:10-32; 17:11-19; John 20; Col. 1:15-18) *God, Revelation and Authority; Covenant and Redemption; Humanity*

3. Jesus' words and acts of compassion provide examples of how God wants us to live. (Matt. 5–7; 22:37-40; Mark 10:13-16; Luke 19:1-10; John 15:9-14) *Discipleship; Rebellion and Sin; God; Community and Church; Ethics and Morality*

4. Jesus' death and resurrection make possible our salvation. (Isa. 53; Mark 15:21-41; John 3:16; 20:1-23; 21:1-13; Rom. 10:9-10; 1 Cor. 15:3-5; 2 Cor. 5:15,18-21) *Revelation and Authority; Discipleship; Humanity; Rebellion and Sin; God; Covenant and Redemption*

5. Through Jesus we know of God's unconditional love for all persons. (John 3:16; Rom. 5:6-8; 1 John 4:9-10) *God; Covenant and Redemption; Revelation and Authority; Humanity*

6. Jesus will return to the earth in power and glory to judge the world and to consummate His redemptive mission. (John 1:51; 14:1-4; 1 Thess. 4:16-17; Rev. 5:9-14; 19:16) *Time and Eternity; Covenant and Redemption; God*

## God: The Holy Spirit

Doctrinal Teachings

1. The Holy Spirit is the Spirit of God. The Holy Spirit is God present and active in the world. (Gen. 1:2, 6:3; Deut. 6:4; Job 34:14-15; Ps. 139:7; Mark 12:29) *God; Sovereignty and Providence; Time and Eternity*

2. The Holy Spirit inspired the writing of the Scriptures and enables people to understand God's truth. (John 14:26; 16:13; 1 Cor. 2:10-14; 2 Tim. 3:16; 2 Pet. 1:21) *God; Revelation and Authority; Faith and Reason; Covenant and Redemption*

3. The Holy Spirit guides people to faith in Jesus Christ as Savior. He convicts of sin, calls to faith, and effects transformation. The presence of the Holy Spirit in believers' lives is the assurance of eternal salvation. (John 3:5-7; 16:7-11; Rom. 8:9-11; Eph. 1:13-14; 1 John 4:13; Rev. 22:17) *God; Covenant and Redemption; Rebellion and Sin; Time and Eternity*

4. The Holy Spirit enables believers to grow in Christlikeness. He cultivates Christian character, comforts, counsels, and helps believers. (John 14:16-17,26; Rom. 8:4-14; 1 Cor. 3:16; 6:19; Gal. 5:16-18,22-23; 2 Tim. 1:14) *God; Discipleship; Ethics and Morality; Community and Church*

5. The Holy Spirit gives gifts to empower the church in evangelism, discipleship, ministry, fellowship, and worship. (Isa. 61:1-3; Luke 12:12; Acts 1:8; Rom. 8:26-27; 12:6-8; 1 Cor. 12:3-11; Eph. 4:11-13) *God; Community and Church; Discipleship*

## God: The Bible, God's Word

Doctrinal Teachings

1. The Bible is the true, authoritative, divinely inspired, eternal Word of God without any mixture of error. (Deut. 4:1-2; Ps. 19:7-8; Matt. 5:18; John 17:17; 2 Tim. 3:16, 1 Pet. 1:25; 2 Pet. 1:19-21) *Revelation and Authority; Faith and Reason*

2. The Bible is the record of God's revelation of Himself to all people. (Acts 2:1-4,32-33; 18:28; Rom. 15:4; 16:25-26; Heb. 1:1-2) *Revelation and Authority; Covenant and Redemption; Humanity*

3. The Bible is God's message for all time. (Isa. 40:8; Luke 21:33; 1 Pet. 1:24-25) *Time and Eternity; Revelation and Authority; Faith and Reason*

4. The Bible focuses on Christ Jesus who is the criterion by which the Bible is to be interpreted. (Matt. 5:17-18; Luke 24:27; John 20:31; Rom. 16:25-26) *Revelation and Authority; Covenant and Redemption; God*

5. The Bible teaches that the way of salvation is through faith in Christ Jesus. (John 20:31; Acts 18:28; Rom. 15:4; 2 Tim. 3:15; Heb. 4:12) *Covenant and Redemption; Rebellion and Sin*

6. The Bible provides guidance for Christlike living. (Ps. 119:11,97-105; 2 Tim. 3:16) *Discipleship; Ethics and Morality; Revelation and Authority; Community and Church*

## God: God's Creation

Doctrinal Teachings

1. God is the Creator of the universe. (Gen. 1-2) *God; Creation*

2. The earth God created reveals His attributes: power (Ps. 104); love (Ps. 136); provision (Matt. 6:25-26); faithfulness (Ps. 146:6); sovereignty (Isa. 40:12-31); holiness (Lev. 11:44; 1 Pet. 1:15-16); wisdom (Ps. 139); grace (Eph. 2:8-10) *God; Creation; Sovereignty and Providence*

3. Discovering God's sustaining power through the natural world can lead to a sense of awe and reverence for God as Creator that can result in worship and faith in Him. (Pss 19; 148) *Creation; Sovereignty and Providence; God; Faith and Reason; Revelation and Authority*

4. Knowledge of God's creation can instill a sense of responsibility for and stewardship of the earth and its resources. (Gen. 1:28; Ps. 104) *Creation; God; Ethics and Morality*

## God: The Church

Doctrinal Teachings

1. The church was established by God within the world, and through the church God is active in fulfilling His redemptive and eternal purpose. (Matt. 16:15-19) *Community and Church; Time and Eternity; God; Covenant and Redemption*

2. The church is the body of Christ and includes believers of all times and in all places. A local group of baptized believers who have been called and gifted by God to do His work in the world is also called the church. (Rom. 12:5-8; 1 Cor. 1:2; 12:17-31; Eph. 1:22-23; 2:19-22) *Community and Church; Covenant and Redemption; God*

3. The church is a fellowship of persons who respond in repentance, faith, and obedience to Christ Jesus as their Savior and Lord and in love to God and to one another. (Acts 2:41-47) *Community and Church; God; Covenant and Redemption*

4. The church is called to follow Jesus' example in its essential functions: evangelism (Matt. 28:18-20; Acts 1:8); discipleship (Deut. 6:6-7; Eph. 4:11-16); ministry (Matt. 20:26-28; 25:31-46); fellowship (Acts 2:42; Eph. 4:2-3; 1 John 1:7); and worship.

(Col. 3:16; Heb. 10:25) *Community and Church; Discipleship; God*

5. The church observes the ordinances of baptism (Matt. 3:13-17; Acts 16:31-33; 1 Cor. 12:13) and the Lord's Supper (Luke 22:14-20; 1 Cor. 11:23-26) to help persons understand and express what it means to be the body of Christ. *Community and Church; God; Covenant and Redemption*

### God: God's Salvation

Doctrinal Teachings

1. God makes salvation known through the Bible. (John 20:30-31; Acts 18:28; Rom. 10:8-11; 2 Tim. 3:15-17) *Covenant and Redemption; Revelation and Authority; God*

2. God is the One who makes salvation possible through Jesus Christ because of His great love for all people. (Ps. 62:2,7; 68:19-20; Is. 43:11; John 3:16; Rom. 5:6-8; 1 Tim. 2:3-6) *Covenant and Redemption; God; Humanity*

3. Salvation is rooted in God's grace and was in His purpose from the beginning. (Gen. 3:15; Jer. 31:33-34; Luke 1:68-69; John 1:1-2,14; Eph. 1:4-14; 2:8-9; Col. 1:15-17,20,22; Tit. 2:11) *Covenant and Redemption; God; Time and Eternity; Sovereignty and Providence*

4. God sent His Son, Jesus, to be the Savior; Jesus' life, death, burial, and resurrection make salvation possible. (Matt. 1:21; Luke 19:10; John 4:42; 1 Cor. 15:2-4; Gal. 4:4-5; Titus 3:4-7; 1 John 4:14) *Covenant and Redemption; God; Rebellion and Sin*

5. God offers salvation to all who repent of sin and trust in Jesus Christ as Savior and Lord. (John 3:16; Acts 20:21; Rom. 10:9-11; Eph. 2:8) *Covenant and Redemption; Rebellion and Sin; God*

### Self: Made in God's Image

Doctrinal Teachings

1. All persons are created by God as His crowning work of creation, in His image, to live and grow in fellowship with Him. (Gen. 1:26-30; 2:7; Deut. 6:5; 1 Sam. 2:26; Ps. 8:3-6; Luke 2:40,52; 1 Cor. 13:11; Eph. 4:15; 1 Pet. 2:2; 2 Pet. 3:18; 1 John 1:3) *Humanity; Creation; God; Discipleship; Covenant and Redemption*

2. God gives persons the freedom to choose to obey or to disobey Him. Because human beings can make choices, God holds us accountable for our decisions. (Gen. 2:16-17; Ex. 20:2-17; Deut. 30:19-20; Josh. 24:14-15; John 7:17; Rom. 3:19; 14:12) *Humanity; Rebellion and Sin; Ethics and Morality; God; Sovereignty and Providence*

3. Because life is a gift from God, persons should act responsibly in caring for themselves and in using the abilities God gives them. (Gen. 1:26-30; 2:15; Ps. 8:3-6; Matt. 22:37-40; 25:14-29; Rom. 12:6-8; 1

Cor. 6:19-20; Eph. 4:11-13) *Humanity; Ethics and Morality; Discipleship*

4. Because God created each person in His image and desires an eternal relationship with each individual, each person has value and human life is precious. (Gen. 1:26-27; 9:6; Ps. 8) *Humanity; Creation; Covenant and Redemption; God; Time and Eternity*

5. Because God created each person for a relationship with Him and other people, each individual finds fulfillment in right relations with God and others. (Gen. 2:18-24; Mic. 6:8; Matt. 7:12; Luke 10:27-28) *Humanity; Discipleship; Community and Church; Covenant and Redemption*

6. Because God appointed human beings to care for the rest of creation (Gen. 1:26,28; 2:15), people should be responsible stewards of God's good earth and the creatures on it. (1 Cor. 4:2) *Humanity; Creation; Ethics and Morality*

### Self: Becoming a Christian

Doctrinal Teachings

1. Every person needs a personal relationship with God. (2 Pet. 3:9) *Humanity; Covenant and Redemption*

2. Every person is a sinner by nature. (Rom. 3:23; 5:12; 1 John 1:8) *Rebellion and Sin*

3. The choice to disobey God (to sin) has negative consequences. (Rom. 5:12; 6:23) *Rebellion and Sin; Ethics and Morality*

4. God has a plan for the salvation of every person. (John 3:16; 1 Tim. 2:3-4) *Covenant and Redemption; God*

5. Salvation is brought about by the work of the Holy Spirit in a person's life. (John 16:7-11) *Covenant and Redemption; God*

6. God saves each person who repents of sin and trusts Jesus as Savior (Acts 3:19; 16:31; Rom. 10:9-10; Eph. 2:8; 2 Pet. 3:9) *Covenant and Redemption; Rebellion and Sin; God*

7. God offers abundant life to all who believe in Him. (John 10:10; 20:31) *God; Covenant and Redemption; Discipleship*

### Self: Living the Christlike Life

Doctrinal Teachings

1. Jesus' life and teachings provide a model for Christian living. (Matt. 5–7; Mark 1:35; Luke 2:52; Phil. 2:5-8; 1 Pet. 2:21) *Discipleship; Ethics and Humanity; Revelation and Authority; Faith and Reason; God*

2. The ultimate goal of the Christian life is to be like Christ as guided by the Holy Spirit (John 14:15-17; Rom. 7:14–8:5; 8:29; Phil. 4:13) *Discipleship; God; Faith and Reason; Humanity; Revelation and Authority*

3. Important elements in Christian living include:

private and corporate worship. (Pss. 96:8; 100:2; 103:1-5; 119:9-11; Mal. 3:10; Matt. 6:5-13; Acts 20:35; 1 Cor. 16:2; 2 Cor. 9:7; Eph. 5:19-20; 6:18; Phil. 4:6-7; 1 Thess. 5:17-18; 2 Tim. 2:15; Heb. 10:25; James 1:22); ministering to others. (Matt. 20:26-28; Gal. 6:10; 1 Peter 4:10; 1 John 3:17-18); witnessing. (Matt. 5:13-16; 28:19-20; Acts 1:8) *Humanity; Discipleship; Community and Church;*

## Others: Family

Doctrinal Teachings

1. God's plan is for the family to be the basic unit of society. (Gen. 1:26-28; 2:18,23-24) *Humanity; Community and Church; God; Sovereignty and Providence*

2. The family symbolizes God's relationship to His children as Father as well as the church in its relationship to Jesus Christ. (Ps. 103:13-18; Rom. 8:32; Gal. 3:26-29; Eph. 4:14-16) *Humanity; Community and Church; Covenant and Redemption; God*

3. God designed the family to be the setting within which religious faith is nurtured and love and service to one another are demonstrated. (Deut. 6:4-9; Prov. 6:20-23; Eph. 4:14-16; 6:4) *Humanity; Community and Church; Discipleship; Ethics and Morality; Sovereignty and Providence*

4. God has given parents the responsibility of establishing a family environment in which Christ is the foundation for mutual respect, love, and learning. (Deut. 6:1-9; Eph. 5:21-33) *Humanity; Community and Church; Discipleship; Covenant and Redemption; God*

5. God commanded children to obey their parents in everything that is pleasing to the Lord. (Ex. 20:12; Prov. 2:1-6; 6:20-23; Eph. 6:1-3; Col. 3:20; 2 Tim. 3:14-17) *Humanity; Community and Church; Discipleship; Ethics and Morality; God*

## Others: Community

Doctrinal Teachings

1. All persons are created by God, in His image. (Gen. 1:26-30; Pss. 8:3-6; 139:13-16) *God; Creation; Humanity*

2. Every person is worthy of respect and love because Christ died for all people. (John 3:16; Rom. 3:21-31; 10:12; 12:9-18; Gal. 3:28; Phil. 2:1-5) *Humanity; Covenant and Redemption; Ethics and Morality*

3. All people are endowed by God with feelings and emotions. That enables them to share in the joys and sorrows of others, and to develop Christlike attachments and commitments. (Ps. 73:21-22; Rom. 12:9-18; Gal. 5:13-14; Eph. 4:29-32 *Humanity; God; Community and Church; Discipleship*

4. People's actions affect one another. This relation-

ship not only calls for purity in life but compassionate response to each other's needs. (Rom. 12:1-21; 14:21; Gal. 6:2,10) *Humanity; Discipleship; Ethics and Morality; Rebellion and Sin; Community and Church*

5. People show love for God and further the cause of Christ by cooperating with others in benevolent ministries. (Eph. 4:11-16; Phil. 2:14-16; Heb. 13:15-16) *Humanity; Community and Church; Discipleship; Ethics and Morality*

## Others: World

Doctrinal Teachings

1. God had a loving plan for the world which included sending His Son, Jesus, to be the Savior of the world. (Is. 7:14; Mic. 5:2-4; John 3:16; 1 Cor. 2:6-10; 1 John 4:9,14) *God; Covenant and Redemption; Sovereignty and Providence; Humanity*

2. God strengthens and guides followers of Jesus to be positive influences for Christ in their world. (Matt. 5:13-16; John 17:15-18; Rom. 12:2; 2 Cor. 1:12; 1 Tim. 4:12) *God; Discipleship; Community and Church; Covenant and Redemption; Sovereignty and Providence*

3. The spirit of Christ compels us to consider the needs of persons (the orphaned, needy, aged, helpless, and sick) and to work with others to meet their needs, always being careful to act in the spirit of love without compromising loyalty to Christ and to His truth. (Gal. 6:10; Eph. 2:10; James 1:27) *God; Humanity; Community and Church; Discipleship, Covenant and Redemption; Revelation and Authority*

4. God helps Christians love persons whose beliefs and practices are different from their own and share faith in Christ with them. (Rom. 14:1; 15:1,7; 1 Pet. 3:15-16) *God; Humanity; Covenant and Redemption; Community and Church*

5. Jesus commanded His followers to make disciples of the people of all nations. (Matt. 28:18-20; John 20:21; Acts 1:8; Rom. 10:12-15) *God; Covenant and Redemption; Community and Church; Humanity; Discipleship*

2. You will find a more detailed copy of this document on KidTrek, the children's Sunday School website, www.kidtrek.com.

Do not merely listen to the word, and so deceive yourselves. Do what it says.
James 1:22

# Chapter 6
# A Model for Teaching
## By Anne Tonks

Miss Bell sat with a group of children telling them the Bible story of Jesus feeding five thousand people. She had her Bible open on her lap and two teaching pictures beside her on the floor.

"One day Jesus was healing the crowds of people who had come to Him," she told the children. "There were about five thousand people. They had been there a long time. Some of them may have come a long way. Jesus knew the people must be hungry. But the disciples wanted Jesus to tell the people to leave.

'They do not need to go away,' Jesus said. 'Give them something to eat.'

Miss Bell paused and picked up one of the teaching pictures. She showed it to the children. "Can anyone tell me what the disciples did next?" she asked.

Miss Bell is careful how she teaches the Bible because she realizes that girls and boys need to know what God says in the Bible. So as she tells a Bible story, guides them through a Bible study, or helps them with Bible application, she is always careful to use her Bible and

In addition to preparing to guide a Bible study, children's leaders must prepare the room, the resources, and the activities. In each leader's guide, instructions for preparing to teach are found near each section or activity. Help is given to locate appropriate teaching helps such as teaching pictures and resources in the leader pack.

help the children use theirs. She frequently uses the phrase "The Bible says . . ." She helps the girls and boys find Bible verses and Bible passages in their own Bibles. Miss Bell feels children need to know God's message in the Bible because they need to:

- learn about God,
- become aware that the Bible is God's message to people,
- develop a biblical value system, and
- learn about and experience love.

Miss Bell also knows that teaching girls and boys is a responsibility God has given her. She must do her best as she teaches girls and boys about Him.

## Preparing to Teach

In order to help girls and boys learn about God and how He wants them to live, children's leaders must begin preparation well before entering the room. As a beginning, each one must be familiar with the format of the leader's guide being used to teach.

70

Each week's material is organized into three major sections called
     Prepare,

         Encounter,

            Continue.

The purpose of the design is to guide the leader, and, ultimately the learner, through an encounter with the Bible passage and Bible truth to an integration of that truth into everyday living.

Prepare consists of Bible study and other actions that will help leaders, both teachers and director, not only discover the Bible truth they will teach the children, but also perceive how the truth applies to their own lives, guiding each of them along the road of a spiritually transformed life. The Bible study is written to lead each reader through a study of the Scripture by reading, answering questions, responding to statements, and praying.
At the completion of the study, the leaders should have been challenged to live out the Bible truth in their own

*Session Schedule*
- **1. Each session begins with a lively group activity.**
- **2. The children then meet as a whole group to focus on Bible study, the memory verse, music, and other Bible-centered activities.**
- **3. For the time remaining, children choose from a variety of Bible-learning activities and challenge projects conducted in small teacher-directed groups. These groups come at the end of the session so that teachers and children can focus on the meaning and application of the Bible truth they have been studying.**

**Writers depend on the guidance of the Holy Spirit to interpret the Scripture in a meaningful way to girls and boys.**

**They must read and reread the Bible passage.**

**They must search through concordances and dictionaries to help with the interpretation.**

**Finally they must be knowledgeable of children and how God made them to develop so that each Bible study helps them know without question how God wants them to live.**

lives. And each teacher in doing so has prepared herself to teach the truths she has learned to the girls and boys. With the help of the Scripture passage and the guidance of the Holy Spirit, she has faced situations in her own life that may need attention. And she has been led to think of ways to guide the children at their level of understanding to know how God wants them to live.

While **Prepare** is a part of getting ready to teach, **Encounter** encompasses the teaching portion of the Bible study. Throughout the section leaders use a variety of teaching activities that help the children become familiar with the Bible passage and the Bible truth contained in it. A lively activity begins the session. The activity captures the attention of the children and introduces them to the concept they will be studying that day.

Next, the director guides the children to form one group. During this time the children may learn and discuss a memory verse, sing, pray, participate in a Bible study appropriate to the age of the child, practice Bible skills, and share in other types of activities that will lead them to understand God's teachings.

During the third portion of *Encounter*, teachers work with small groups of girls and boys as they begin to think through ways they can apply the Bible teaching in their own lives. Leaders intentionally offer activities that will meet the needs and interests of the girls and boys and familiarize them with what God wants them to know.

**Continue** is the portion of the weekly material introduced during the latter part of **Encounter**. While **Continue** is introduced during the teaching portion of the session, the implementation extends throughout the coming week. Through a variety of activities, children learn ways they can apply the Bible truth. The leaders' responsibilities also extend throughout the next week. Suggestions in the leader guide under **Continue**, provide the leader with a variety of ways to reinforce the Bible teaching in the lives of the girls and boys as well as in her own life.

As designers and writers structure the curriculum, they make sure that in every **Encounter** the following points are an integral part of the Bible study. Read the following section several times. Make the questions and statements a part of your thinking. Then every week as you read and study the Bible passage and teach the children, use the questions and statements as a guide.

- **Acknowledge Authority** : *Who or what is the authority in control of my life?* (Control)
  A leader should approach the study of each passage by first determining what authority, power, or rule guides his life. In the light of each Bible passage, the reader should examine prayerfully the condition of his own heart and life.

**Although the points listed are not marked where they appear in the curriculum, they will each be a part of the design of every session.**

- **Search the Truth:** *What historical setting and key words are reflected in the content of this Bible text?* (Content)
  The leader should discover what God was saying when He sent the message to the people who first received it. What were the circumstances in which the message was given? What did the message mean to them?

- **Discover the Truth:** *What eternal concept is the Holy Spirit revealing to me from this Scripture?* (Concept)
  Under the guidance of the Holy Spirit, the reader must endeavor to find the message or truth contained in the passage and begin to understand it in a personal way.

- **Personalize the Truth:** *In my life context, what is God teaching me personally from this Scripture?* (Context)
  Next the reader must ascertain what the truth means in today's world; and move from there to discern what the truth means in his own life.

At this point some children may begin to ask questions about salvation. Leaders should be sensitive to comments and question children may have about becoming a Christian. Helps for talking to a child are found in *Good News for Kids* by Cindy Pitts.

- **Struggle with the Truth:** *What conflict or crisis of belief is the Holy Spirit bringing about in my heart and life?* (Conflict)
  Because most of the time truth is not an easy thing to face, the reader must answer questions such as: What life questions, problems, issues, or struggles compel me to seek answers and promises in the Bible?

- **Believe the Truth:** *What new biblical conviction is God leading me to integrate into my life?* (Conviction)
  After struggling with the previous issues and questions, the reader now accepts the truth and where the Holy Spirit has led him to realize it fits into his life.

- **Obey the Truth:** *How is the Holy Spirit changing my conduct in how I think, what I value, and the way I live?* (Conduct)
  The culmination of the process comes to rest with the action or actions the leader has realized he must implement in his life. This is the climactic point of the Bible study. This is where a life can be transformed into the kind of life God wants each person to live.

In addition to searching and personalizing the Bible truth for herself, a teacher of children must also determine how the Bible truth relates to the lives of the children she teaches. As the teacher works through the Bible study and leads the children through the session, she prayerfully and constantly seeks God's direction. Hopefully, she knows the children well enough that she is able to determine what effect the teaching of a specific Bible truth could have in the life of that child. Hopefully, she will understand that the process is a spiritual one and will rely on the leadership of the Holy Spirit to implement the changes in the lives of the children.

**HANDS ON**

Now that you know how the sessions are structured and how their content is treated, take your leader's guide and see how many of these sections you can locate. Choose a session and fill in each blank space with the appropriate information.

Unit title:

Session Date–Week of:

Session Title:

Bible Passage:

Biblical Setting:

Biblical Truth:

Key Bible Verse:

Life Question:

Life Impact:

## Guidance for Getting Ready to Teach

The first step in preparing to teach is to become familiar with the Bible passage. Read the verses; now read them again. Read some verses on either side of the passage. Use commentaries, concordances, and Bible dictionaries to give you information and insight. Find geographical locations on a biblical map of the period. Ask God to help you find the truth in the passage and help you apply it, first to your own life, then to the lives of the girls and boys you teach.

As you study, listen for the Holy Spirit. Be aware as He presents God's message and applies it to situations in your life. Then think of the children you teach. What is happening in their lives? What are their families like? their

**To enhance your Bible study, use a *Disciple's Study Bible* or look in your own Bible for some of the recommended helps.**

homes? How do they get along with the other children? What aspect of the Bible study will speak to a particular problem in a child's life? As the Holy Spirit touches your heart through God's Word, be open to ways you will help the children understand and apply the message.

Each hour of Bible teaching is divided into three parts. The first part, takes place as the children enter the room. Leaders immediately involve the children in a dynamic activity that introduces them to the subject of the Bible study. Activities are designed so children can join in as they arrive. The activity may be directed by any combination of teachers and director. One person must be available at the door to greet the children and guide them to join the group, as well as record attendance.

After about ten minutes, the children move to the second segment of the session. The director will lead this part of the session. Teachers and children may be seated in a semi-circle or other appropriate configuration. Children are guided through a variety of activities, all of which are related to the Bible study. Activities may include Bible skills, a Bible study or story, a Bible application story, activities with a memory verse, music, prayer, and other activities that reinforce the Bible study. This section is designed for approximately 25 minutes.

The third part of the hour-long session is designed to help children look more closely at the Bible truth and begin to think of ways they will apply it in their own lives. The director offers several choices to the children and children meet in a small teacher-directed group.

**Choices offered to children include two activities outlined in each session and additional activities such as two-, three-, or four-session Challenge Projects found in the Leader Pack.**

As you plan each session, keep these questions in mind.
- What truth do I want the children to learn from this Bible study?
- What will they learn about God?
- How can this Bible study change their lives?
- How can I help them apply the truth to their lives?
- How will each activity lead them to the Bible truth?
- Will one activity help them reach their goal better than another?

# Characteristics of

| Family Bible Study | Bible Foundations |
|---|---|

## Bible Study Plan

Includes a balanced study of Bible books, doctrine, history, and classic passages

Study plan organized around biblical worldview categories and addresses life issues

Organized around Bible topics that help build foundations for faith

Emphasizes Bible study, missions awareness, and discipleship

## Bible Study Approach

All ages use a common Bible study theme with common passages as often as possible

Children study passages suitable for the the age group

## Publishing Cycle

Dated and released quarterly

Dated and released quarterly

## Age Grouping

*Closely Graded*
(1-2, 3-4, 5-6)
*Broadly Graded*
(1-3, 4-6)

Broadly Graded (1-3, 4-6)

## Bible Translation

*Closely Graded*
New International Version Memory verses in NIV
*Broadly Graded*
Memory verses in NIV and KJV

Based on New International Version
Memory verses in NIV and KJV

## Leader Resources

*Closely Graded*
Separate Leader Guides and Leader Packs for grades 1-2, 3-4, 5-6
Leader Packs include CD-ROM with songs, sound effects and leader helps
Teaching pictures sold separately
*Broadly Graded*
Single Leader Guide and Leader Pack Grades 1-6
Leader Packs include CD-ROM with songs, sound effects and leader helps
Teaching pictures in Leader Pack

Single Leader Guide and Leader Pack for Grades 1-6

## Learner Guides

*Closely Graded*
Magazine format with 26 "Church" pages and 26 "Home" pages perforated for easy removal
Pages include interactive activities to reinforce the biblical truth in class and at home
*Broadly Graded*
Magazine format with 26 "Church" pages and 26 "Home" pages perforated for easy removal
Pages include interactive activities to reinforce the biblical truth in class and at home

Magazine format with 26 "Church" pages and 26 "Home" pages perforated for easy removal
Pages include interactive activities to reinforce the biblical truth in class and at home

## Devotionals

*Closely Graded*
Separate devotional guides: *More* (grades 1-2); *Adventure* (grades 3-4); *Bible Express* (grades 5-6)
*Broadly Graded*
Separate devotional guide: *Adventure* (*More* and *Bible Express* also available)

*Separate devotional guides: More (grades 1-2, Adventure (grades 3-4), Bible Express (grades 5-6)*

# Weekly Plan Sheet for Family Bible Series or Bible Foundations

As you plan each week, check each item on the list.

Prepare

_____ Complete the Bible study.

_____ Gather needed items and prepare the room.

_____     _____

_____     _____

_____     _____

Encounter

_____ Study **Plug In** or **Get With It!** and make notes here.

_____     _____

_____     _____

_____ Study **Power Up** or **Get Into It!** and make notes here.

_____     _____

_____     _____

_____     _____

_____ Study **Personalize** or **Go With It!** and make notes here.

_____     _____

_____     _____

_____     _____

_____ Determine which actions you will take under **Continue**.

_____     _____

_____     _____

For everything that was written in the past was written to teach us, so that through endurance and the encouragement of the Scriptures we might have hope.
Romans 15:4

# Chapter 7
# Learning and Doing–
# Real Experiences, Simulations, and Learning Centers

## By Chris Ward

What are the two things that children do best when they come to us? Talk and move. Yet some adults continue to think children are only learning if they are quiet, sitting still, and all doing the same thing at the same time. While whole-group learning is one of many effective ways to learn, children learn best by doing and by being actively involved in each learning experience. A child can be listening quietly yet be mentally active and engaged in the Bible truths being taught.

Learning about God should be a hands-on and minds-on experience. Children need challenges and exposure to a wide variety of teaching strategies that are designed to meet their individual abilities and interests.

## Real Experiences

Amanda, along with the rest of her second-grade Sunday School department, has been studying about church leaders. Last week, the children discussed the questions they wanted to ask the pastor and the teacher wrote them down on a chart. Each child chose one of the questions to personally ask the pastor during this morning's visit to his office.

"How in the world could Bible people play music from this thing?" asks Terrence as he examines a curvy ram's horn. "And why is it called a *shofar*?"

The boys' mission group spent a busy Saturday morning at the local food bank sorting canned goods, peanut butter, rice, and beans into boxes. They know their efforts mean that food will now be ready for immediate delivery to hungry people.

In the above examples, children are involved in real experiences. They are applying in authentic ways the Bible truths and Scriptures they have learned. Field trips, sensory explorations, and involvement in ministry are ways that children's learning can be enriched and personalized. Learning that is internalized and remembered over time occurs when the child is doing, seeing, hearing, and feeling.

## Field Trips

A field trip is a learning experience that takes a child outside the classroom to see firsthand what is happening or to hear a person share his experience. Children can read about church leaders, write about church leaders, discuss what they know about church leaders, and will come away with an understanding of what it is like to be a church leader. However, nothing can take the place of visiting with the pastor, interviewing him, and getting a sense of his world. Such a genuine learning experience completes the learning package and gives children the fullest possible picture of church leadership.

Teaching suggestions found in Southern Baptist Sunday School, discipleship, music, and missions literature for children incorporate a variety of learning styles. Such an approach assures that the needs and interests of all children will be met throughout each session.

Field trips should be carefully planned to enrich the learning experience. Appropriate field trips include visiting different areas of your church such as the baptistry or the library; finishing a study of creation with a nature walk or a visit to a park, orchard, or aquarium; learning how Jewish people worship by visiting a synagogue; seeing mission activities in action by visiting a mission, a food bank, or the Red Cross.

## Preparing for the Field Trip

For children to get the most out of a field trip, prepare well ahead.

- Notify parents several weeks in advance. Here is a sample letter that might be sent.

To the family of Christian,

The First Grade Sunday School Department will be visiting Harriet Wheelon, a shut-in, during Sunday School on July 29. We are putting into action one way to help people as Jesus did.

We are asking that each child bring a piece of fruit on Sunday, July 29. We will make a fruit basket to take to Mrs. Wheelon.

Please sign below to give your child permission to be transported in teachers' cars. You are welcome to join us! Thank you!

First-Grade Teachers

- When necessary, obtain permission notes with parent's signature.
- Arrange transportation.
- Be sure there is a good adult/child ratio for adequate supervision. Let adults know their role and responsibilities during the trip.
- Visit the location to meet the person who will be leading the tour or speaking with the children. Let her know what you expect and find out exactly what the children will be doing. You may find the site is not what you thought or is not age appropriate.

Preparing the Children

To assure the fullest possible learning experience, the children also need to be prepared for the trip. The teacher should include the children in the process.
- Discuss the purpose for the field trip.
- Let children take responsibility for their learning. Ask questions such as:
     What do we know about the subject?
     What do we want to find out?
     How could we find out those things?
- When the place for the field trip is chosen, help children compile a list of questions. Let each child choose a question to ask on the trip.
- Discuss expectations for good behavior for the trip and while being transported.

Take the Trip
- Assign a small group of children to each adult for supervision and support.
- Take pictures or make a video recording during the visit, if appropriate.
- Guide children to ask their questions. Should other question arise as the visit progresses, guide children to ask them or answer them yourself.

Following the Trip
- After the trip, highlight all that was learned. Identify what was seen and heard and have children share their feelings.

- Document the learning with pictures, a class book, a photo essay, or reports.
- Write a thank-you letter to adults who helped with the trip.
- Charts are ways children can report the information they discovered. One type of chart to use is a K-W-L chart.

**Under K, the children write (or the teacher records what they say) What We Know.**

**Under W, the children list What We Want to Find Out.**

**After the field trip the children list under L What We Learned.**

## Sensory Experiences

Experiences that involve children's senses make learning come alive. If you have never eaten an apple, a picture of an apple cannot convey its taste, smell, variety, or texture. You do not truly know an apple until you have eaten one. Sensory experiences should be integrated into teaching to enrich each child's learning.

Cooking and tasting activities can help children experience the foods and customs of Bible times. Olives, nuts, unleavened bread, dates, figs, fish, honey, grapes, and dried fruit are examples of foods eaten in biblical days. To broaden their understanding of life in Bible times, children may sample small portions of these foods or prepare an entire meal.

Sensory experiences that involve music appeal to auditory learners. Children can make their own cymbals, horns, shakers, and tambourines and use them to act out some Bible stories. Playing the Autoharp helps children know what David's harp was like.

Children should be encouraged to touch and explore items that relate to the Bible teaching. For example, a sheaf of wheat can help children understand Ruth's task of gleaning the grain. One teacher brought *denarii*, ancient Roman coins, for the children to see and compare to present-day coins. Woven baskets, clay pots, sewn cloth, and fishermen's nets all inspire curiosity. Nature items such as cotton bolls, animal homes (shells, nests, hives), and biological specimens (snakes in a jar!) provide concrete learning opportunities for children.

**Be sure to provide lots of magnifying lenses to encourage examination!**

## Involving Children in Ministry

Involving children in ministry is a real experience that enables children to put the Bible truths they are learning into action. Mission action involves girls and boys on many levels by requiring their thought, feelings, and participation. While some ministry actions might involve leaving the church premises, there are many opportunities to work on site. Children can make or collect ministry items and adults can deliver them. Notify parents in advance if items from home are needed.

Teachers can help children consider ways to minister as needs arise within the church, in the community, or in the world. When hurricanes or tornadoes damage areas around the country, boys and girls can help gather cleaning supplies, clothing, and food. Other ideas include:

## Hospital Ministry.
Children can make tray favors that feature Bible verses, record audiotapes of stories or poems, create cards, and cut up drawings for puzzles.

## Food for the Hungry.
Children can decorate a box with cutouts, drawings, and pictures. Canned goods and nonperishable items can be collected.

## Neighborhood Ministry.
Organize older children to rake leaves, wash cars, clean out garages, and attend to other needs.

## Toys Ministry
At Christmas, children are thinking a lot about the gifts they hope to receive. Guide them to consider the lives of less fortunate families and have them bring in a new toy for a needy child.

## Homeless Ministry
Collect toiletry items such as toothbrushes, toothpaste, and tissues for delivery to the closest homeless shelter. If your church has a homeless ministry, involve children in making and serving a meal.

## Simulations
Simulations involve children in representing a Bible story or event so they feel as if they are there. A church in our city transforms the bottom level of their building into the city of Bethlehem during the Christmas season. From real sand on the floors, palm trees, and camels, to tent homes and fresh fish for sale in the market, you feel as if you are walking through Bethlehem at the time of Jesus' birth. Such a simulation provides a personal experience as well as a meaningful connection to Bible times.

Many Bible stories and events, such as Noah and the flood, can be simulated right in the teaching room. Guide children to bring stuffed animals from home and arrange

**HANDS ON**

Think how you and your children might create a simulation of Jonah and the whale or Joshua and the city of Jericho. Write here some of your ideas.

*Exploration Station*
Activities and suggestions to set up a learning station are found in leader packs for the Family Bible Study for younger, middle, and older children.

an "ark" out of the chairs. Darken the room and add sounds of rain and thunder. The children can be Noah and his family on the ark with stuffed animals everywhere. A child or teacher could narrate the story.

Take a temple tour to help children learn who Solomon was and what the temple may have looked like. Plan a trip to the church sanctuary imagining it to be Solomon's temple. The teacher is the tour guide and leads the children around the temple describing it and sharing facts. Then the children can conduct a worship service.

A museum simulation can be used in different content areas. One group planned and created a museum depicting various historical forms of the Bible. The exhibit displayed the Bible in various forms—a storyteller, clay tablets, a scroll, a handwritten book, a printed book, an audiocassette tape, and a CD-ROM. As visitors came to the museum, children told about the different displays.

At Christmas, children can plan a living Nativity simulation and invite others to visit. Lengths of cloth, head bands, and scarves can transform children into Mary, Joseph, the shepherds, and angels. Again, input from the children ("How can we show baby Jesus?") is important. When children see their own ideas in place, learning is more personalized.

## Learning Centers

Say-Chun is in a corner of the room looking at all the choices of activities under a large banner that says: "Meet Some Women in the Bible." The teacher explains some of the activities to him and he thinks for a moment. He chooses to illustrate a page for a book on this topic, gathering poster board and markers. Say-Chun remembers the Bible story last week about Deborah and decides to make her the focus of his book page.

Caitlin is trying to determine which center to choose in choir. She finally decides to go to the table where she will make her own tambourine. Next week she'll be able to practice on the Autoharp, her second choice.

*Learning centers* are areas where small groups of children can work independently to discover more about a particular topic. Various activities can be housed in one learning center to help children learn a particular Bible truth. Since we know children have preferred learning styles and learn using multiple intelligences, it is important to provide areas where children can learn at their own pace. Children who prefer a little quiet time and who like to pursue answers to questions on their own find these needs met through learning centers.

*Learning center* activities are prepared ahead of time by the teacher and may be used for early arrivers to become involved in learning immediately. Learning centers can also be used as one of many options for choice in the room. Since children finish activities at different times, learning centers provide extensions of learning. If children are not given opportunities and choices when they finish a task, they will find other ways to use the free time and behavior problems may arise. Learning centers can be used to reinforce, further develop, and enrich a topic, Bible skill, or idea.

*Learning centers* will usually have many activities available to children that pertain to the Bible theme. Teachers include crossword puzzles, word searches, games, Bible activities, map and globe activities, art activities, open-ended stories, and many other possible ideas. All supplies children need should be in place at the learning

**These research resources should be available in every room.**

Bibles
Bible dictionaries
Bible storybooks
Missionary stories
Encyclopedias
Concordances
Maps (current and Bible times
Commentaries
Standard dictionaries
Bible word lists
Pronunciation guides
Outdated teaching pictures

center including research supplies, musical instruments, art materials, and pencils. The computer can also be used effectively as part of a learning center. Activities can refer to a particular Bible person, to the unit being studied, or to fostering Bible skills.

*Learning centers* may be located in various places in the room. Use a table, the floor, a desk, or a corner. Keep the learning center inviting with activities that are fun and relevant to the ages and abilities of the children. A learning center is a place where every child should find success. Activities need to span a range of levels to meet the individual needs of each child. Learning centers can be an effective teaching method in a multi-age group.

The teacher's role is to prepare the materials and activities for the learning center with the needs and abilities of the children in mind. The learning center should be ready for children who arrive early and the teacher should be in place to greet and guide children. Younger children will need more support and guidance from adults. The teacher should observe the children's progress at the learning center and offer help as needed.

*Learning centers should:*

- be planned to meet specific learning objectives
- include activities that can be completed in a reasonable amount of time
- build and expand upon learning and past experiences of each child
- create interest and stimulate active learning
- provide for the needs, abilities, and differences in learning
- accommodate children with various capabilities and challenges
- spark curiosity, discovery, and exploration
- encourage creativity and imagination
- promote problem solving, peer interaction, reasoning, and questioning

## My Challenge

Plan to teach the girls and boys in your department the best way you can. Read back through the chapter and choose two methods that you have seldom or not used before. Plan to incorporate them into your teaching this year.

Do your best to present yourself to God as one approved, a workman who does not need to be ashamed and who correctly handles the word of truth.
2 Timothy 2:15

# Chapter 8

# Learning and Doing-Research

## By Chris Ward

Research is a way of finding information to answer a question or develop an activity or project. The results of that search should be shared with others in ways that motivate children. When children are excited about the way they have decided to share their findings, they will be more motivated to research.

Jonathan and his group are planning a large map of Paul's first journey. They use their quarterlies, maps of Bible times, and the Bible to help them record Paul's travels on their map.

Justin wants to know what the Ark of the Covenant looks like. He and his teacher find pictures of the Ark in a Bible storybook and in some teaching pictures.

Claire is preparing a diorama about Esther and Mordecai. Since her diorama will be on display in the church library, she looks for information in her Bible and resource kit materials to write on an attached label.

Children need resources at their fingertips in order to find the information they need. Research tools include books, pamphlets, videos, audiotapes, computers, pictures, magazines, newspapers, charts, and maps. Other sources, such as travel brochures for pictures of the Holy Land, might also be appropriate. A variety of material is available in learner guides, leader packs, and teaching pictures. Excellent research tools are included in the back of most Bibles, such as word lists, time lines, maps, and interesting information about the Bible itself.

The three most common types of research that children use to learn more about God and Bible truths are historical research, survey research, and descriptive research. The choice of the type of research will depend on the questions children are asking and the information they are trying to obtain.

## Historical Research

Historical research is the most common type of research children use to find answers to questions about something that happened in the past. There are many ways for children to find and share such information, including oral histories, time lines, maps, and interviews.

## Oral Histories

Some information is not recorded in books, resource kits, or videos. Personal accounts and stories are within the memories of the people who experienced them. Oral histories are the telling of these stories to others. For example, one of the best ways for children to learn more about missionaries might be to listen to a local missionary "tell his story". Oral histories add a much more personal aspect to learning than might be found in books. Children may tape record the oral history so that the story not be lost and other children might learn something from it. Oral histories can be catalogued and kept in the church media library.

Other ways that oral histories might be used include:
- Listening to an older member talk about the church's earlier days
- Listening to an accomplished musician tell how he learned to play his instrument
- Listening to a nursery worker share her story of caring for infants and watching them grow

## Time Lines

A time line is a chronological ordering of events or time periods that helps children see the relationship of one event to another. A time line can be constructed using line (wire, string, yarn) on which cards with dates and events are attached. A time line can be drawn on paper or made on the wall with a line of masking tape. Younger children can draw a picture for each event and place the events in the correct order.

Time lines may be used to review what happened in a Bible story, such as Daniel and the lion's den. The time line might contain these cards:
1) Daniel was very wise.
2) The king wanted to make Daniel ruler of all the land.
3) Other wise men were jealous.
4) Daniel prayed to God.
5) The jealous men went to the king and tricked him into making a new law.
6) The new law said you must pray only to the king or be thrown to the lions.
7) Daniel prayed to God anyway.
8) The king had to throw Daniel to the lions.
9) The next morning, Daniel was alive.
10) God saved Daniel by sending an angel to close the lions' mouths.

Time lines may be used to relate events during a certain Bible period or in the life of Jesus. The life of a Bible person or a missionary can be depicted through a time line. Even the history of your church or church leaders can be shown through a time line, as well as the history of the Bible.

A variety of research tools can be used to gather information for a time line. Here are some suggestions for using time lines effectively:

- Events should relate to the unit or topic being discussed.
- Prepare a card or sheet for each event. On each card, children can write the date and a brief description of the event. Pictorial time lines are good for nonreaders.
- A clothesline time line that spans from corner to corner of your room can be fun.
- Each event or time period should be discussed as children look for information and sequence the cards.
- Guide children to decide the best way to share what they have learned with others.

## Map Making

Making maps inspires children to research information from the Bible, maps, and other sources. Learning about the difficulty in the travels of Bible people long ago becomes more real when children reconstruct the journeys on maps of their own. Children learn much more about the Jerusalem of Jesus' day when they make a map with its walls and temple. Maps related to mission work help children understand the distances missionaries travel to tell others about Jesus.

**Map making is a fairly abstract activity and more developmentally appropriate for older children. Young children cannot visualize distances and have difficulty transferring understanding to a map.**

Children can make many types of maps with different materials. Maps can be drawn on butcher paper with crayons and markers. A large flat bed sheet can be used for a map children create with markers or paint pens. A canvas floorcloth makes a wonderful floor map. Children enjoy planning three-dimensional maps made of salt and flour, cornstarch, or clay mixtures. As children plan their maps, they need research tools handy. Maps can be found in quarterlies, in atlases, in Bibles, and in leader packs. The church library can be helpful in finding specific maps.

To support children in their map making:

1. Choose the map to be copied. Use research materials to find the map that best depicts the content being studied.

2. Decide what type of map to make. Children can decide if the map needs to be simplified, enlarged, flat, or three-dimensional.

3. Decide what landforms, cities, and other locations will be on the map. Discuss with children the Bible story or unit and review the locations that are important. Make a rough sketch of the map. This will serve as a plan or blueprint for the actual map.

4. Create the map. Whether on paper, cloth, or cardboard, children will draw the outline, using their blueprint for guidance. If the map is a three-dimensional clay mixture, a sturdy piece of thin plywood or cardboard will be needed for its base. The clay or salt/flour mixture will fill in the outline and harden over a few days so features can be added. Children can form the clay mixture to show the different elevations in the region. For further definition of locations and regions, portions of the clay mixture can be dyed using food coloring

5. Add the details. Different colors can be used on flat maps to show different locations, as well as various elevations. Highlight travel routes, such as Paul's journeys, with different colors for each journey. Yarn can also be used to depict routes. Include names of cities, regions, and locations by labeling directly on the map or by making signs or toothpick flags. Permanent markers work well on canvas, but protect children's clothing with old shirts.

6. Learn from the map and share the learning with others. Discuss the meaning of the map and have children express what they have learned in their own words. Guide children to see the relationship between one location and another, using relevant examples. Children can figure distances using the map scale. Compare travel in Bible times with travel today. Would Paul journey the same way today? If the map is of a building like your church, talk about the ministries in each area. Help children think in new ways about life in Bible times, Bible lands and locations, and the work of missionaries.

Other ways to consider making maps:
- Make a map of the sanctuary as if you are on the ceiling looking down (bird's eye view).
- Make a map of Jerusalem in Old Testament times and compare it to Jerusalem in New Testament times. Trace the travels of missionaries from your area.
- Make a map of your state mission work.
- Use push pins on a map of your city to mark sites of mission work . Attach yarn to each pin with a card on the other end explaining the mission action.
- Follow the path the Israelites took to Canaan.

98

# Interviews

Interviews are an excellent way for children to gather information about events that happened in the past, as well as in the present. Sometimes historical research requires talking to someone who can tell us about the past. Interviews provide a way to find out information through questions and conversation. Since most children like to talk, interviews are a popular way to do research. However, children need guidance from adults for effective interviews to occur. An entire department can be involved in interviewing or a smaller group of children can interview someone and share the information with the others. Interviews can be conducted within the church building or may require a field trip offsite.

To conduct an interview, children need some way to record the information they will hear. Boys and girls can take paper and pencils to jot down notes, but this is difficult even for adults. A cassette recorder is an easier way to document the information from the person the children are questioning. Children can listen to the conversation again as a group and stop the tape to ask questions. Or an adult can record the entire interview with a video recorder to be seen and discussed later by the group.

The following suggestions will help prepare children for a successful interview:

* *Help children plan the interview.* Children need help knowing the right questions to ask. Sometimes younger children need practice asking questions, rather than making a statement or telling a story. In planning for the interview, guide children to ask: What is it we want to know? Who has experience in this area and could answer our questions? When would we conduct the interview? Guide children to list the questions they want to ask.
* *Set a date with the person to be interviewed.* Let the person know the kinds of questions to expect. Take time to talk with the person so you feel the interview will relate to the unit topic or Bible truth you are studying.

- *Determine where the interview will take place.* Be sure the location will comfortably accommodate all the children involved. If possible, check out the site yourself first. On a visit to the pastor's office with my first grade Sunday School class, a child bumped into a coat rack by the door. It fell, narrowly missing the other children. Had I been more observant, I would have moved that coat rack out of the way before the children arrived.

- *Decide who will do the interviewing.* Children may take turns asking questions taken from the list they generated. The interview can be conducted by a whole class, but try to keep every child involved. Any child who wants should be able to ask a question. Prior discussions should have prepared children to ask thoughtful questions. A few children can conduct the interview and report their findings to the whole group.

- *Conduct the interview.* Be sure each child has a question to ask from the list. After they have been asked, children might have other questions. Often, the person being interviewed will talk about an area you had not considered, so spontaneous questions will arise. Thank the person for the time and information.
- Share the interview. Children need time to discuss what they learned from the interview. Determine the best way to document the information gained. The children can report what they learned by compiling a class book, organizing the information on a chart, or other appropriate ways they might suggest.

Some suggestions for using interviews in historical research include:
- Talk to an older member of the church to find out how the church has changed over the years.
- Interview a teenager who has made a profession of faith. Ask what led her to make such a decision and how her life is different now. Children have many questions they will want to ask, because some of their friends are beginning to make professions of faith.

- Find a missionary or former missionary who will tell children firsthand experiences of ministry in the field.
- Interview the minister of music about the history of some of the musical instruments.

## Survey Research

When children want to find out information from a group of people or research how people feel about an issue, then survey research is appropriate. While not used as much as other types of research, survey research serves a purpose and can yield information other types of research cannot. The type of research used depends on the questions children are trying to answer. For example, if the questions that arise are: "When did children in this church learn to pray? Who helped them learn?", a survey would be an excellent tool. Older children could devise a simple survey form with adult help, make copies, and distribute them to another Sunday School department. The results would give children some insight into prayer from their peers' perspective.

Survey research is suited for older children, with adults guiding the process. However, if the question requires a yes/no answer, young children can make tally marks in columns and conduct a simple survey themselves *Did you bring your offering to Sunday School? Yes/No).* Younger children can also respond to a question by placing stickers under the appropriate column. *Were you kind to others this week?*
*...most of the time      sometimes      not at all.*

Be sure to plan the survey well ahead of time.
- Discuss with children the best way to answer the questions they are posing.
- Decide whom you will survey. Keep the number small and manageable.
- Prepare a simple survey together with just a few items so it will not take long to complete. Make enough copies to distribute.
- Determine how you will get the surveys returned to you and set a due date on the survey.

- When the surveys have been received, decide with the children how to record the information.
- Discuss the results; are they surprising in any way?
- Share the results with others.

Other ideas for using survey research are:
- Survey parents to find out why they attend the church.
- Survey church helpers to find out their duties, how long they have been a church helper, and how they feel about what they are doing.
- Survey a class of older adults. What do they wish every child could know?
- Survey peers to find out family habits such as reading the Bible, bringing an offering, and family devotions. Why are these habits important? Children might find other unique ways in which families bring God into their homes.

## Descriptive Research

When children find information by observing an event or a way of doing things, they are using *descriptive research*. They watch what is going on and describe what they observe. Children then report their findings to others in a manner best suited to the group. Findings can be shared orally, discussed as a group, or written down in a log or journal. For example:

- During a study of God's creation, the second grade Sunday School group decides to adopt the huge oak tree outside their window. They will keep a diary in the window, and each week a child will record an entry. *What is happening with God's tree? How does it look this week? Do I see anything different about it?*

- The missions group observes the church puppet team practice their skits and monologues. To add depth, the children also interview a member of the puppet team about her role in ministry and worship.

- While learning about the Lord's Supper, the children observe the deacons prepare the trays of bread and the cups of grape juice. The following Sunday, the children observe the Lord's Supper during the worship service.

Charts can be used with all types of research to help children organize their information. Simple T-chart surveys can be on a large piece of paper or poster board so all can see and respond. Another type of chart is a "Then and Now" chart that compares and contrasts some aspect of Bible times with the way we do things today. In a "Who? What? When? Where? Why?" chart, a Bible passage can be analyzed with responses under each of these columns. The children can compile charts with words and their definitions.

Whether a child is creating a skit or making a Bible person puppet, he will need to do some research in order to find information. Older children have more experience using various research tools such as books, encyclopedias, and Bibles, so the teacher can facilitate and guide the research process. Younger children will need additional help and guidance. Plan to use picture books and play Bible games to learn facts. Simple picture Bible dictionaries are also helpful. Part of the research process is knowing where to look for different information.

## My Challenge

Plan to practice some of the new skills you have read about in this chapter. Work on one at a time. Encourage your fellow teachers to work with you. Remember that teaching about God is so important that you must tray many approaches to meet the needs and engage the interests of the girls and boys you teach.

I will instruct you and teach you in the way you should go; I will counsel you and watch over you. Psalm 32:8

# Chapter 9
# Activities that Teach-
# Art and Drama

## By Chris Ward

My favorite teacher wears a pin like no other I have ever seen. A small orange feather sticks out of the top of a lopsided piece of corrugated cardboard. Small kernels of popcorn are glued in the shape of a crooked heart, with sequins scattered around. Pieces of tissue are wadded into tiny balls and attached around the edge. She loves people to ask her about the pin; she calls it her "creativity" pin. It was a gift many years ago from her then seven-year-old daughter. She had made it after spending an afternoon rummaging around and finding odds and ends in the kitchen drawers. The pin is a cherished possession to my friend; a symbol of the spontaneous creativity that is waiting to be discovered within each child.

Creative activities provide an outlet for children's emotions and thoughts. We can see the unique child God created when she is expressing herself creatively through art, drama, music, or creative writing. All children are creative in delightfully individual ways. Teachers must uncover those abilities and encourage children to make the most of them.

# Art

Art is experienced differently by a child than by an adult. When adults look at works of art in a museum, they view the product in all its beauty. When people look at a masterpiece by Van Gogh, they do not think about all the troubles he was enduring while he painted it. In children's art, however, it is the process that is essential. The thoughts and feelings that caused the child to express herself the way she did are much more important that the end product. Children speak to us in more than one hundred languages if we will but listen and give them the opportunity. Art is one way for children to communicate their thinking and emotions with us—it is a powerful and revealing language from the child's heart.

**A creative person has the ability to invent, generate ideas, and approach problems in unique ways. Creative children show persistence, an ability to shift from one idea to another, interest in new ideas ("What if....?), and a tendency to make insightful observations.**

Why is art such an important avenue for children to share their learning about God? Art experiences tap into the affective area of learning and give children opportunities to have their feelings affirmed. In addition, art:
- develops creative thinking
- provides a means of communication and self-expression
- serves as a balance to other classroom activities
- develops appreciation of the individuality of others
- strengthens self-concept and confidence
- enhances the ability to visualize
- provides problem solving and decision making opportunities
- serves as an emotional release
- meets individual needs, abilities, and learning styles

The type of art being discussed is creative art—art that comes from within the child. (Sidebar: One teacher calls children's art the "hands off" experience.) The rule for adults is to supply the materials for the children, stand back, and see the unique creations unfold. The teacher becomes the observer, the listener, and the one who believes in the child's ability. Then she can be the encourager, and guide, and the one who helps the child believe in himself. Now the child is free to be inventive, searching, and daring in his creative efforts.

Children will approach art openly and without inhibition, especially when they are younger. But sooner or later, adults who mean well begin to interfere with the child's art process. Comments like, "Here, let me draw it for you.", "Color the sun yellow, not red.", and "I don't think your picture is finished. Put something else on it." tell children that their efforts don't quite measure up. Instead of being more open and creative in their art, children begin to become more dependent on others for their ideas and to doubt their own abilities.

Art can become a special privilege for a teacher when he stops trying to direct and control the activity so the child will end up making some sort of pre-conceived product. Creative art is not tracing pattern pieces for children to cut and paste together to look like an adult model. Creative art is not coloring within the lines. If you look at children's art and it all looks the same, that should tell you something is wrong. Didn't God make each of us a unique and special individual?

I had observed Miranda paint a beautiful scene complete with blue sky, several trees, birds, a turtle, the sun, and what looked like a horse and two people in the center of the picture. When I moved beside her, she said, "See? It's Adam and Eve and all the things God made." I commented on all the bright colors she used in her painting and moved over to another child. A few moments later, I turned and saw Miranda covering her wondrous creation scene with heavy globs of black paint. Stifling the impulse to stop her, all I could say was "Wow!". She smiled at me and said, "Now it's nighttime 'cause God made the dark too."

God made a diverse world. Children should be able to reflect that in their art, but are often restricted by the materials offered. I'll never forget Shanghenk, a Laotian girl, sorting through the construction paper and saying, "There is no paper the color of my face." Today there are multitudes of art materials available to rectify the situation. Markers come in varying shades of skin colors, from golden tan to ebony. Tempera paint, tissue paper, and construction paper are sold in shades to reflect the diverse skin tones in our world. Hopefully, the church would be the one place children could count on to feel included and have a sense of belonging. Even if your children are similar in culture and race, they should have access to diverse art materials.

## Drawing

Drawing is as basic to children as breathing. With only limited materials required, drawing is an opportunity for every child to share in the learning process. Children need room to draw, so larger pieces of paper should be provided. Newsprint, rolls of computer paper, shelf paper, and butcher paper are excellent for drawing. Using colored chalk, children can draw on sidewalks outdoors. Provide markers, pencils, crayons, colored pencils, and pastels for drawing experiences.

Some ways drawings can be used include the following:

- *Diptych.* (DIP-tik). A diptych is made by attaching two panels of paper or poster board together. Each panel may have pictures, or one side may have words to a prayer or song. A Bible verse may be on one side with an illustration of how that verse applies to our lives on the other. Diptychs are often used for "Then and Now" comparisons.

- *Triptych.* (TRIP-tik) A triptych is similar to a diptych except it has *three* panels. A triptych can be folded with all panels containing drawings or combinations of drawing and words. A Bible truth may be written on the middle panel (How can I Help Others?) with illustrations on either side.

- *Accordion-fold Pictures.* Accordion-fold pictures are made by taping several pieces of paper or cardboard together so that the strip of pictures folds and unfolds. This method helps children sequence a story. For example, the Bible story of Joseph from beautiful coat to bondage can be told through a series of pictures.

- *Frieze.* A frieze is a series of separate pictures related to one theme or idea. Children work on separate pictures, but plan them together. For example, children might plan a frieze about Jesus' miracles, discuss what miracles to include, and then choose one to draw.

- *Story Strip.* A story strip is a sequence of pictures drawn by children with conversation balloons included. Older children especially enjoy this method of sharing their feelings about a subject or showing what they have learned about a unit theme.

- *Overhead Projector Drawings.* Children draw on transparency film with permanent markers (wear protective clothing). Then they share what they have learned with everyone as they project their drawing on the wall using an overhead projector.

- *Printing*. Using a variety of techniques, children's drawings can be printed onto another piece of paper or cloth.

(a) *Sandpaper Prints*: Give each child a sheet of sandpaper. Ask the children to draw heavily on the sandpaper, using crayons only. Place the sandpaper drawing-side down onto white paper. Iron the back of the sandpaper.

(b) *Styrofoam Tray Prints*: Place a thin layer of thick paint in a tray.Children will draw on another tray with a sharp object such as a pencil or pen. This will make indentations in the styrofoam. Using paint brushes or rollers, guide children to spread paint on the entire surface of the tray drawing. Press immediately onto white or light-colored paper. Several prints can be made from one application.

(c) *Cloth Prints*: Have each child plan his drawing first on a piece of paper; then guide the child to draw the picture on paper using fabric crayons. Provide each child with squares of cloth (about 12" by 12") and place the paper drawing-side down onto fabric. Iron with medium heat. The drawing will be transferred onto the cloth mirror style, so avoid using words. The cloth squares can be used to make a quilt or wall hanging related to a Bible theme.

## Painting

The bright colors of paint provide another medium in which children can draw. Children enjoy using tempera paints, poster paints, and watercolors to express themselves and to show what they have learned.

Large pieces of paper are needed to give children the independence they need to paint freely. Butcher paper, drawing paper, and construction paper are good choices. Protect the table with newspaper and be sure children wear paint smocks (men's shirts with the sleeves cut off work well). Provide a variety of good quality paint brushes that include both wide bristles and smaller detail brushes. In addition to brushes, children enjoy painting with feathers, cotton swabs, roll-on deodorant bottles, and toothbrushes. Keep cleanup supplies, such as wet paper towels and sponges, nearby.

Various types of surfaces can be used for painting. Each surface provides a different feel and result. For example: construction paper; newsprint; tissue paper; tin foil; cookie sheets; plexiglass; mirror; wood; cardboard; paper tablecloths; paper bags; waxed paper; trays (metal, plastic, styrofoam); table surfaces; boxes; sand paper; paper towels

- *Individual Paintings.* Children can paint pictures to show how they feel about a topic or theme or to highlight their learning about the Bible (Joshua's life, ways to minister to others, the Ten Commandments, ). Children in my first grade Sunday School department enjoy choosing their favorite Bible story and illustrating it with watercolors.

- *Murals.* A mural is a large painting or pictorial design. that is a cooperative effort centered around an idea or theme. Children can plan and paint a mural about God's creation, using music to praise God, or Jesus' birth. Wide paper that comes in rolls, such as freezer or wrapping paper, works best. Children can use a variety of media, such as paints, markers, chalk, or crayons. Branches, yarn, cotton balls, cloth, and pipe cleaners add a three-dimensional effect. Children will need to plan the mural and have resources available to do research. Based on the research, children will come up with a list of the main facts to be reflected in their mural.

- *Posters.* Posters give children a chance to present an idea simply and in a way that will catch the eye. While poster board is most often used, cardboard, cloth, burlap, felt, and wrapping paper offer variety. Simple illustrations and bold lettering will give the poster appeal. Posters can be created to highlight the unit topic (Women of Courage in the Old Testament), advertise an upcoming event (Children's Choir concert), or to let people know about mission projects.

- *Montage.* A montage is a design made with pictures and words related to a single idea. The pictures and words may be cut from quarterlies, magazines, and newspapers, or drawn and printed by hand. The pictures and words are glued on paper or poster board so that they overlap without the background showing.

- *Collage.* A collage is a design made with pictures and words that are related. Cellophane, fabric trimmings, tissue paper, corrugated cardboard pieces, and yarn are some items that might be used on a collage. Pine cones, twigs, pebbles, and other nature items would be suitable for a collage showing God's creation.

- *Modeling with clay.* Clay modeling is another way for children to share what they have learned about God. Various types of non-hardening clay can be used, as well as types that harden overnight. Clay figures can represent Bible people or objects. Clay can be combined with other materials for table scenes, dioramas, maps, or displays. Clay can be used to make objects used in Bible times such as pottery or tablets representing the Ten Commandments.

## Scenes

- *Scene.* A scene is a three-dimensional representation of a location or event. Scenes can be planned for tabletops or placed inside boxes. Children enjoy planning Bible scenes together, although an individual child who prefers to work alone can make a smaller scene, for example, inside a shoebox. Scenes can be based on Bible stories, lives of missionaries, church activities, or present day applications of Bible truths. The scene should relate to the theme being studied.

Materials will vary with the type of scene. Children will enjoy using their imagination in using several materials. Pipe cleaners and craft sticks can be adorned with pieces of cloth to make people. Small boxes and milk cartons can be buildings; while straw, cellophane, cotton balls, paint, construction paper, and clay objects can be added for details. Some of the many types of scenes children can make are dioramas, peep boxes, and table scenes.

- *Dioramas.* Dioramas are scenes displayed in a shoe-box, paper box, or even a refrigerator box. The box is turned on its side and children design the background scenery and the event or site itself. Figures of people can be held in place with modeling clay.

- *Peep Boxes.* A peep box is similar to a diorama except that a hole is made in one end of the box to peek inside and view the scene. The box lid is kept on, but an opening can be made and covered with cellophane to give a skylight effect.

- *Table-top Scenes.* A table-top scene is good project for a group of children to work on for several sessions. The table provides easy accessibility, particularly for a child in a wheelchair. Table-top scenes provide room to depict neighborhoods and geographical regions.

## Mobiles

Mobiles are pictures and arranged forms that hang suspended from the ceiling using wires or yarn. Interest is drawn to a mobile as air currents cause the pictures and forms to move and turn. A *stabile* is similar to a mobile, but the forms and pictures are attached to a stand instead of the ceiling.

Children can make mobiles in many ways. Twigs, branches, straws, wire hangers, and strips of poster board can be used for hanging forms with yarn, thread, or string. Older children will enjoy planning mobiles with many pictures or forms that require a delicate balance. Mobiles and stabiles can be used to involve children in learning in the following ways:

- Illustrate ways to show love on paper hearts.

- Provide shapes and write Bible verses on one side of a shape and draw an illustration on the other side.
- Show how instruments in Bible times compare to instruments today.

## Drama

Drama involves children in acting out situations, facts, personal experiences, stories, and ideas. When children are involved in drama, they think first about the person they are portraying. By discussing the feelings of that person and other background events, children learn to put themselves into the "shoes" of others. Drama causes children to think and become more sensitive to the emotions and resulting behavior of others.

Dramatic presentations help Bible stories come alive for children. It provides another avenue for learning and sharing about God for those children who are kinesthetic learners. As children dramatize the life of a missionary, they begin to understand the hardships and commitment involved. Drama helps children apply Bible truths to their own lives as they dramatize the way God would have them act in given situations. Role-playing situations help children discuss possible consequences and solutions to problems.

- *Monologue.* In a monologue, a child "becomes" another person and speaks from that person's point of view. Monologues help children learn about the life and work of other people. Based on research about the Bible person, missionary, or church helper, the child gives a first-person account. "Hello! My name is Matthew and I am one of Jesus' disciples." The monologue may be read aloud very simply or a more elaborate monologue with props and costumes may be planned.

- *Dramatic Interview.* A dramatic interview is different from a regular interview because the child being questioned pretends to be another person. The children involved need resources to research and write interview questions and answers. Dramatic interviews can be conducted in several ways. Children can interview as a group. A panel can be interviewed ("Today we have with us Mary, Martha, and Lazarus. They have agreed to answer a few questions."). Or the interview can be one-on-one. Children enjoy interviews because they can pretend to be newspaper reporters or TV anchor persons.

- *Picture Posing.* Picture posing is a very simple form of drama and an effective way to introduce drama to children. Very few materials are needed for picture posing—simply a picture and children to pose it. Unit teaching pictures are excellent for picture posing. Children pretend to be the characters in the picture, and imitate their expressions and stances. When a teacher gives the signal, the children involved hold the pose for a few seconds. Thought and discussion about the picture is encouraged through questioning as children prepare for picture posing.

- *Tableau Posing.* Tableau posing is similar to picture posing, but is a scene very carefully posed with costumes and props. The scene may be based on a picture or originate from a Bible story or a present-day situation. For example, children may re-create the events of Jesus' resurrection by posing the Last Supper, Jesus praying in the garden, Jesus carrying the cross, and visits to an empty tomb, all as part of the tableau.

- *Pantomime.* Pantomime is drama without words. Children are very familiar with this form of drama. Boys and girls act out situations, Bible stories, and ways to apply the Bible verse. An adult can serve as a narrator and read the Bible story as the children act it out silently. Costumes are not necessary, although children may decide to include simple props and costumes. Choose stories to pantomime that involve a lot of movement and action. For example, Jesus praying on the Mount of Olives might be better suited for picture posing, while Jesus feeding the multitude could involve several in pantomime. Other ideas for pantomime would include dramatizing choice-making situations, mission stories, jobs of church helpers, and a church worship service.

- *Role Playing.* Role playing is a spontaneous drama based on a Bible story or a specific situation or problem under discussion. Children take on the roles of the characters and act out the story. No script or costumes are necessary as children work in an impromptu manner. Through role play, children learn to understand the feelings of others and to apply Christian beliefs in various situations. Role play can also be used to introduce or to review a Bible story, to bring family issues up for discussion, and to show the consequences of different types of behavior.

- *Puppet Drama.* In puppet drama, children take on roles of characters through puppets. For many children, this is an easy way to present a drama because attention is focused on the puppet. Puppets can be used in monologues, to act out present-day situations, and to dramatize Bible songs and verses. Any story can be told using puppets. More important than making the puppets themselves is the research and study in

**The purpose of music is participation, not performance.**

preparation for the drama. In presenting the puppet drama, simple puppet stages can be made from the following materials:

—boxes

—large paper bags

—towel draped over an arm

—towel draped over the back of a chair

—a table turned on its side

—a sheet held by two friends

Puppets can be made from almost any material. Some suggestions are:

—cloth attached to a tongue depressor

—paper sacks stuffed with newspaper

—flyswatters

—socks stuffed with newspaper attached to a stick or left unstuffed for a hand puppet

—papier mache puppets

—coat hanger pulled into an oval or round shape and covered with a nylon stocking

—oatmeal box attached to a dowel

—feather duster

—a mop head

—plastic bottles

—wooden spoons

—garden gloves

and on and on.

Shout for joy to the Lord, all the earth. Worship the Lord with gladness; come before him with joyful songs.
Psalm 100:1-2

# Chapter 10
# Activities that Teach-
## Music, Creative Writing, and Learning Games

### By Chris Ward

## Music

Music is inside each of us, yet many adults feel uncomfortable integrating music into their teaching because they "can't sing!" Children, on the other hand, enjoy musical experiences and are not the least concerned with their abilities. They believe they have music inside them and want opportunities to share an expression of joy.

If adults think of music in terms of performance, they feel less comfortable encouraging music with children. The purpose of music is participation, not performance. Adults could take a lesson from children's natural, relaxed approach to singing and playing instruments. Singing off-key and playing off-rhythm are accepted as each child joins the joyful chorus praising God's name.

When choosing songs to sing, it is not necessary to have great ability. But it is important to choose appropriate songs. Here are some guidelines to help in the selection process.

- *The song relates to the content of the unit theme.* Since most teachers are with children a very short time each week, it makes sense to use the time wisely and sing songs connected with the topic at hand. Fun songs about holidays and other subjects unrelated to the unit theme are better sung at other times. Even the best songs, if unrelated to the biblical truth being discussed, use time that could be spent in better ways.

- *The song contains words that children understand.* Printing the words of the song on a chart or using large, computer-generated text can be helpful in discussing the meaning of a song. Role playing what the song means and its application to their lives is another helpful method for children. Difficult words can be explained. Younger children are literal thinkers, so songs that avoid symbolism are better choices.

- *The song has a melody that is easy to sing.* It is not an enjoyable experience to try to screech out a song that is too high, to follow a song with a complicated rhythm, or to growl a song that is too low. Try to choose songs with simple melodies that fall within the range of most children. Children like catchy tunes that are fun to sing. When you learn a new song, sing it several times during the the unit so it becomes familiar to the children.

- *The song is scripturally true and doctrinally sound.* Music is simply another teaching method. Songs teach Bible facts, Scriptures, and ideas. Children remember songs much longer than words they have heard. Be sure the songs you choose support the biblical message and the doctrine of the church.

Activities incorporating music include the following:
- *Antiphonal singing.* Two groups of children engage in antiphonal singing by alternating parts of the song. Simple songs with repeating phrases work best. Children can write their own words to a familiar hymn and sing it antiphonally.

- *Rounds.* Children enjoy singing songs in rounds, songs in which phrases are repeated. One group begins the song; another group begins after one or two phrases, and so on. Several groups may participate. A short song works well in rounds, because children like to repeat the song several times.

- *Playing Musical Instruments.* Children enjoy playing musical instruments and it enriches their experience. As people in Bible times praised God with instruments, children can worship and honor God in the same way. Children can learn to play simple songs on the Autoharp. Resonator bells are appropriate for group activities, with each child receiving one bell and one mallet. Rhythm instruments—rhythm sticks, cymbals, wood blocks, sand blocks, and triangles—can be used by children to accompany hymns of praise. Children can write their own songs to play on a zither.

  Children can easily make simple musical instruments of their own. A shofar, or ram's horn can be made from a cone-shaped piece of poster board. Simple shakers can be made by lacing together two styrofoam plates, first placing beans or rocks in between the plates. Other ideas for making instruments are:
  —*Drums.* Make drums out of empty coffee cans with plastic lids, plastic ice cream pails, or oatmeal boxes. Children can decorate with paper, paint, or markers.
  —*Cymbals.* Make cymbals out of tin foil pans. Attach a string for handles.
  —*Canister shakers.* Fill film containers with rice, sand, rocks, or beans.
  —*Tambourines.* Attach small jingle bells to foil plates.
  —*Rhythm sticks.* Use dowel rods or wooden spoons.

- *Listening.* Listening to songs and hymns helps children learn new songs and think about their meaning. Listening to hymns is part of Christian worship and should be modeled for children. As children listen quietly to new or familiar songs, they can pray silently or search for facts and ideas in the verses.

- *Rebus.* A song rebus is a word chart of a song with some of the words replaced by pictures. Children can illustrate the rebus with their own pictures or cut pictures out of magazines. A rebus is an excellent way to teach a new song.

- *Illustrating Songs.* When children illustrate a song, they think about the meaning of the words. Children can work individually or as a group to illustrate phrases of the song. As children draw, play the song so they can listen as they work. Song illustrations can be shared with others by using a mural or frieze or compiling the pages into a big songbook or accordion style format.

- *Writing Original Songs.* Children can express feelings and originality when they write their own songs. They can write new lyrics to a familiar tune or make up their own melody. Original songs express praise, worship, and thanksgiving. As a means of closure to a unit, an original song can demonstrate the child's understanding and feelings about biblical truths learned.
  While most adults don't consider it music, many children would be motivated to write an original song if it could be a rap. Relax and let it happen!
  My name is Chris and I'm here to say
  Let's praise and worship God today!

- *Hymn Studies.* Wonderful hymns are a part of our Christian heritage. Older children need exposure to singing and studying great hymns and learning about the composers. Provide resources for research after choosing a hymn to study that is related to the unit goals. Be sure there are enough hymnals for children as they listen to and sing the hymn. Find basic facts about the hymn and its composer, including its important teachings. Continue to give children opportunities to study the hymns to be used in special worship services such as Christmas and Easter.

## Creative Writing

Writers of all ages write best when they have meaningful reasons to write. Children should not write to please adults; but to express their feelings, ideas, and how they think. Would it surprise you to know that many children are unable to write due to fear of failure? Some children cannot express themselves on paper because they are trying to use only the words they can spell correctly. Others cannot focus on the content of their writing because they are trying to make it perfect. And they know they will probably just get one chance to get the punctuation right!

If teachers want children to feel good about their writing, they must provide an environment that allows risk taking. Children should be encouraged to put their ideas and feelings on paper, using whatever skills they have. The mechanics of writing—punctuation, spelling, and hand-writing—are skills that children will continue to perfect.

Writing materials should be organized and accessible on shelves. Markers, pencils, a stapler, tape, notepads, a variety of paper, envelopes, glue, tape, paper clips, crayons, and a computer are items that can contribute to a child's creative writing experiences. Types of creative writing include the following.

- *Letter Writing.* Writing letters is a form of creative writing in which children can convey their feelings. Children may work as a group to write one letter or work alone on individual letters. Letters are usually written to real people, but can be written to an imaginary person. Some examples for letter writing include:
  —writing a letter to a church helper thanking them for the work they do.
  —writing a letter to a missionary on his birthday.
  —writing letters to children who have not attended church for a while.
  —writing a Bible person and asking him questions

- *Diaries/Journals.* Diaries and journals are personal expressions of feelings and experiences. Writing in a diary or journal is an excellent way for children to develop courage and confidence. A child pretending to be a missionary, Bible person, church helper, or an imaginary person may write a diary or journal. Other ways to use diaries and journals include:
  —keeping a journal, making entries about what it is like to be a new Christian.
  —using a worship diary to include descriptions of worship experiences.
  —preparing a diary from David's point of view.

- *Learning Log.* A learning log is similar to a journal in which a child makes regular dated entries. However, a learning log is a place for children to write down facts and information they hear about a topic. For example, in a unit about worship, children might use their learning logs during each session to record the main facts they have learned about worship. Learning logs can be used to write down the main ideas of the sermon, to take notes about different composers, and to note the applications of a Bible story.

- *Newspaper Writing.* All children are familiar with the newspaper. In newspaper writing, children concentrate for several sessions on writing articles about a particular subject. The newspaper can be printed by hand, or a computer with desktop publishing can make the task easier. Either way, children need to be involved in the decision making and in writing at least one article. Older children are able to assume the responsibility involved with newspaper writing, although younger children can certainly put together a simplified version with support.

Examples of ways to use newspapers:
  –Plan a newspaper based on the current events of your church.
  –Plan a newspaper to involve children in learning about Moses' life.
  –Plan a newspaper to report on the various ministry efforts of the church

- *Story Writing.* When children write a story, it gives the reader insight into how the child is thinking and understanding the topic. Story writing allows a child to express herself in unique, creative ways. Children should always be encouraged to say things in their own words. Younger children can dictate their stories to an adult who only writes the child's words (even though it is tempting to clean up the grammar or correct the story in some way).

Stories about Bible times and biblical principles can be compiled and shared with others. Teachers of younger children can make "Big Books" with their stories, books large enough so that all can see during a shared reading time. Words that children dictate can be typed and enlarged using the computer. When "Big Book" pages are laminated and compiled using metal rings or plastic binding, they can be placed in the

class library area where all the children can enjoy them. Examples of "Big Books" written by younger children include:
—The Life and Times of Moses
—The ABC Creation Storybook
—Our Favorite Bible Stories
—Women in the Bible

- *Poetry*. Poetry is a method that helps children examine their feelings and emotions about God and Bible truths. While children seem to focus on poetry rhyming, teachers can help them see that the thoughts in the poem are more important than forcing the words to rhyme. Children benefit from hearing poetry read aloud before they start writing their own poetry. The book of Psalms is rhythmical in its message and an excellent example of biblical poetry. Some types are:
—*Cinquain*: A poem that follows this pattern:

One word title
Two words that describe the title
Three words that express an action
Four words that express a feeling
One word that is another word for the title

David
Musical     Brave
Praying  Praising  Loving
Ruler who loved God
King

—*Haiku:* a Japanese poem that contains seventeen syllables and does not rhyme.

Title
Five syllables
Seven syllables
Five Syllables

Resurrection
The stone rolled away
He has saved me from my sin!
Yes! He is risen!

- *Mind Mapping or Webbing.* Mind mapping or webbing combines both visual images and information. Research has shown that the brain remembers patterns more easily than linear images, such as rows of words or paragraphs. Webbing can be used to take notes, remember information, and gather ideas for creative writing. The topic or subject area starts in the middle of the paper. Like a spider web, lines extend outward with questions or subcategories to explore. Brainstorming ideas causes the web to expand.

- *Litanies.* A litany is a prayer written so that a repeating response line alternates with lines of praise. Children write the litany, then a leader or child will read the praise lines and the entire group will say the response lines. One of the best ways to familiarize children with litanies and prepare them for writing is to study a litany from the Bible. Psalm 136 is a good example.

  Response lines determine the focus of the litany. Some examples of response lines are:
  —We thank you, Lord.
  —Lord, we praise you.
  —Here my prayer, O Lord.  (Psalm 143:1)

- *Riddles.* A riddle is a puzzle or a problem stated in the form of a question. Children love to try to come up with answers to riddles and enjoy writing their own. A riddle contains clues and will usually end with a question such as "Who am I?" "Where am I?" or "What am I called?"

  Riddles can be used to review a unit theme, to introduce children to Bible people, or to familiarize children with various musical instruments. Riddles can be written to help children learn the duties of different church helpers. Children enjoy writing riddles about themselves, which helps adults and other children get to know them better. Riddles can be shared one line at a time, with children trying to guess as the clues get more specific.

I did not obey God.
He asked me to go to Ninevah and
tell the people to stop their evil.
I got on a big boat to try to run away from God.
I ended up in a big fish.
Who am I?
(Jonah)

- *Biographical Sketch.* A biographical sketch is a brief account of a person's life. Research is required for the child to compile the most important facts about the person. A biographical sketch is usually short, one or two paragraphs. Encourage children to use the appropriate type of research for the sketch. Interviews are suitable for church helpers, family members, and local missionaries. Other research resources need to be available for writing about Bible characters, composers, or mission efforts in the state.

- *Script Writing.* Scripts are written for dramatizations and contain the dialogue of the characters involved. A script is basically a plan for the drama. Children can write the entire script or use notes to help guide them in their presentation. Scripts can be used with puppets, monologues, or to dramatize a Bible story. Children can write scripts for teaching pictures or their own illustrations and tape record them in advance, then play the recording as the pictures are shared.

- *Brainstorming Wall.* Using a poster or large chart, children write words or phrases describing a subject or feeling. For example, in the middle of a large piece of paper is the word "Prayer." Children respond in writing by brainstorming the first ideas and thoughts that come to them. After the paper is covered with ideas, children's thoughts about prayer are discussed and summarized. The teacher can then build upon these ideas and integrate them into the teaching.

A variation is "Carousel Brainstorming," where several sheets of paper are hung around the room with a question at the top of each. The questions are related to the Bible study theme. Children are placed so that just a few are in front of each station. At a signal, children have 2-3 minutes to respond to the question, writing their thoughts on the paper. When time is up, a signal is given and children "carousel" in a clockwise fashion to the next station and repeat the process. They may not all answer in the same way, so they read what is on the sheet and brainstorm new and different responses. This process encourages children to go beyond easy responses and search for extensions of their thinking. When they have visited all the stations, the groups can discuss and synthesize the responses to each question.

## Learning Games

Every child loves to play games. Games and puzzles have been a part of children's lives since the beginning of time, and there seems to be no indication that this interest in games is diminishing. Electronic games and computer games are best sellers, yet even the simplest games still capture children's interest and attention. The

most genuine games may be those that children invent themselves.

Learning games can be as educational as they are fun. Social skills of negotiation, turn-taking, listening, sharing, and being a good leader can be fostered in learning games. Bible truths and unit ideas can be reviewed and reinforced. Because games motivate many children, enthusiasm for learning can be encouraged.

When selecting or creating games for children, keep game rules specific and simple. Complicated rules and intricate games will detract from learning that should occur. Discuss the rules beforehand, so all have an understanding of how to play. Try to emphasize cooperation rather than competition. If playing in teams, guide team members to help one another in answering questions. That helps shy children or those who have missed some sessions. Emphasize learning rather than winning.

Leader packs provide many games for use and commercial games can be a springboard to further ideas. Classic games like tic-tac-toe can be adapted in suitable ways for church groups. Children may have good ideas for new games or modifications of old ones.

In addition to the various types of games played in groups, children enjoy creating and solving puzzles. Word searches, crossword puzzles, and codes are an excellent learning tool for early arrivers and those who finish tasks early. Puzzles can be used to help review Bible facts, learn Bible verses and information as a part of research, and to introduce children to a new topic.

- *Review Games.* Review games are used to help children remember facts and information from previous learning. As games are used to review, the ideas and applications are reinforced. Review games may be played in teams or by individuals. Some review games involve the whole group, yet will not be played in teams.

130

For example, Toss the Beanbag is a fun way to review unit content. The teacher begins by asking a question. Children who think they know the answer hold out their hands. The teacher tosses the beanbag to one child. If the child answers correctly, he asks the next question and tosses the beanbag to a child who knows the answer.

- *Team Games.* Team games should have simple rules. Playing "fair" is important to children, so abide by the game rules that have been agreed upon. Review games are usually played with equal teams. While children like pitting girls against boys, it usually leads to intense competition and may cause problems. Assign teams in a variety of ways—according to colors worn, by counting off, or by assigning half of the semicircle to one team and the other half to the other team.

  Many team games and game boards are provided in the leader packs. Game boards that feature topical, seasonal, and sports themes can be used over and over simply by changing the questions.

  A tic-tac-toe grid can be placed on the floor using masking tape. Children can answer each question as a team and then place markers on the floor grid. If left on the floor, children can choose the game as an early arriver or early finisher activity.

  A four-square grid with a number in each square (1-4) provides a game board that can be used in a variety of ways. Children can toss a beanbag onto the game board. The number of the square where the beanbag lands is the point value of the question.

- *Individual Review Games.* Individual review games are played by one child at a time and do not involve competition. Winning is less of an issue, as each child usually chooses the individual review game he will play or has control over his own responses. Some games for individuals include:

**Laminating game boards will preserve them for future use.**

—*Puzzle Match:* Children try to match two-piece puzzles that contain information related to the unit theme. For example, children can match a Bible verse to the picture that shows its application; Bible characters can be matched to a Bible fact; music terms can be matched to pictures that illustrate the terms.

—*Memory:* Children enjoy playing this game (also known as Concentration) alone or with friends. Using pictures or word matches, children turn over two cards at a time to find a match. As pairs are found, they are removed from the game. For example, church helpers and their duties might be the topic of a memory game.

—*Puzzles*: Children can make their own puzzles by cutting apart outdated teaching pictures.

—*Who Said It*?: Write statements made by the Bible characters on conversation bubbles (cartoon balloons). Children can match it to the appropriate Bible person.

**Puzzles can be stored in envelopes.**

—*Clue:* Write clues on a piece of paper or use small items. Children draw them from a box or can and tell how each is related to the unit of study.

- *Information Games.* An information game helps children learn specific facts. All the information the child needs to learn is included. The games help children master information in a way that is fun, challenging, and interesting. Information games can be used to introduce new content as well as support learning in other sessions. Information games include matching, codes, crossword puzzles, scrambled words, mazes, and word searches.

Some other information games are:
   —Bible Verse Match: Print each Bible verse on a different color paper. Cut each verse in half, like a puzzle. Give each child one half of the verse and place the other half on the floor. Children match their verse and try to read it (suitable for younger children).
   —*Order the Verse:* Write the Bible verse on a sentence strip. Cut each word and the reference apart. Distribute a card to each child in mixed-up order and let the children reorder the verse. *Variation:* Let each child hold a card and guide the other children (audience) to put the children holding the cards in order.

* *Bible Skill Games.* Teaching children how to use the Bible is a skill practiced repeatedly as children grow up in the church. When choosing skill games, consider the age and individual abilities within the group. Be sure the focus of skill games is on practicing the Bible skill and handling the Bible with reverence. The purpose is always on learning, not on rewarding winners.

   Be sure each child has access to a Bible. Bibles should be kept on shelves in each room. Children should be encouraged to bring their Bible to every session, and in doing so, leaders have the responsibility to use the Bibles. (Sidebar: Many churches now annually present Bibles during the worship service to each child entering the first grade, thus modeling the belief that the Bible is indeed the best book.)

Bible skill games include:
* *Books of the Bible Games:* These games help children learn the books of the Bible. (Not recommended for younger children.) One version divides the group into two teams, with each team receiving a stack of cards containing the books of the Bible. The cards should not be arranged in order. Each team tries to 1. Sort the cards according to Old Testament and New Testament, 2. Arrange the Old Testament cards in order, and 3. Arrange the New Testament cards in order. Each of the three events can be timed. The

team successfully completing two out of three events is the winner. Children use their Bibles throughout the game, as appropriate..

- *Matching Games*: Create games in which children match a key passage with its accompanying reference (Matthew 5-7 matches the Sermon on the Mount).

- *Bible Application Games*. Application games help children think about how Bible truths apply to their present-day situations. These games may not have specified answers, but instead ask the child to consider how they might react in different scenarios. Children can also write responses in their diary or journal before discussing with the group.

- *Agree or Disagree*. A scenario is read and children share whether they agree or disagree with the statement. Ask children to support their opinion and discuss the Bible principle being applied.
  Jessie knew she needed to have good grades in order to go to the slumber party on the weekend. On her last math test, she received a low grade. Her teacher gave her a note for her parents to sign. Jessie decided to give the note to her parents on Monday, after she went to the slumber party.
  Agree or Disagree?

- *What Would You Do?* In this game, the child tells what he would do in a given situation and suggests a Bible verse to support the choice.
  Matt and Jonathan are best friends. The teacher introduces a new student, Mark, and asks Matt and Jonathan to sit by him at lunch and introduce him to their classmates. Mark is in a wheelchair. Matt tells Jonathan,
  "That guy is weird. He is never going to be our friend!"

  If you were Jonathan, what would you do? What Bible verse would help?

- *Choice and Consequences.* In this game, children can begin to anticipate the various consequences to their actions. Given a situation, children should list various choices and the possible consequences of each choice. As in life, the scenarios should include some examples that do not involve absolute right and absolute wrong.

Daniel and Brent were walking down the hall on their way to class. Daniel nudged Brent so that he tripped and fell. Other students laughed at Brent, causing him to be embarrassed and upset.
"It was an accident! Someone bumped into me first," Daniel said.
Brent was sure Daniel had bumped him on purpose.

What are Brent's choices? What are the possible consequences of each choice?

Apply your heart to instruction and your ears to words of knowledge. Proverbs 23:12

# Chapter 11
# Studying the Bible with Children

## By Anne Tonks

Chelsea and Jonathan are working a memory-verse puzzle about loving others. Miss Jones talks to them about ways they can show love to their friends and family members.

The preteens have divided into groups and are looking for Bible passages that tell about the wonder of God. As they find and read the verses, they fill in words on a giant crossword puzzle.

The Bible Drill team practices every Sunday afternoon. The girls and boys are getting very good at locating and memorizing significant verses and passages in the Bible.

The main function of children's workers in the church is to help children know and understand God's message in the Bible. Girls and boys can learn through a variety of approaches and methods what God wants them to know. But the purpose of teaching children God's message in the Bible is to help them understand and apply that message in their own lives. workers need to employ a variety of appropriate Bible study approaches in order for God's message to make a difference in the lives of girls and boys.

**Children's curriculum provides a multitude of suggestions to guide children in Bible study and learning.**

# Using Bible Verses with Children

Memorizing Bible verses has long been an important part of what children do at church. But that is only a beginning. Children need to learn the meanings of verses as well as their words; then put those meanings into practice in their daily lives. They need to be able to recall a meaningful verse at appropriate times long after their first exposure to it. The goal of guiding girls and boys to learn Bible verses is for them to find God's way for their lives as well as to instill in them a love and respect for God and His Word. Here are some guidelines.

**Learning that will remain with a child involves more that a one-time use and interpretation of a verse.**

- *Children absorb new material gradually.* Generally speaking, the younger the child, the fewer the verses she can be expected to learn and relate to her daily life.
- *Children differ in their abilities.* Just as some children learn to talk or walk earlier than others, so some can memorize words and grasp meanings more quickly.

**Repeat! Repeat! Repeat!**

- Children learn by repetition. The more often a Bible verse is used and recalled, the better he will remember and apply it. To keep the child interested in learning, methods used should be varied and engaging.
- Children's learning is greatly enhanced when they are involved in the learning. Singing a verse, acting out the meaning of a verse, matching verses with present-day pictures, and other age-appropriate activities, help children learn God's message.

**Comment on how well a child is learning the Bible verses. Help him know when he is implementing a Bible truth.**

Avoid giving rewards such as stars or candy for learning verses. Such a strategy may appear effective in the beginning but eventually will be counterproductive. When rewards are no longer offered, the child may not bother to learn the verses at all. Giving of material rewards will minimize the positive influence Christian adults can have in the lives of girls and boys.

For older children who have trusted Christ as Savior as well as children who are not yet Christians, laying foundations for Christian conversion should begin in early childhood through a consistent study of selected Bible verses and passages. Particularly in the preteen years, it is important that girls and boys understand God's message. Allow time during Bible study sessions for preteens to ask questions and express their understanding of Bible verses and passages.

# Helping Children Develop Bible Skills

Younger Children (Level 1)

First and second graders are primarily occupied with learning to read and write. They do not need the added burden of memorizing Bible books and divisions as well. When children have completed the second-grade, they should be able to:

- Know that certain stories and verses are in the Bible.
- Recognize the Bible as a book from God.
- Name and locate the two main divisions of the Bible, the Old Testament and the New Testament.
- Be able to locate certain books in the Bible and be familiar with what they contain. For example:
  —the Book of Genesis tells about God and His creation
  —the Book of Psalms contains songs about God
  —the Book of Luke tells about Jesus
- Locate the contents page in their Bibles. Be able to locate books containing the memory verse, the Bible story, or the name of a Bible person
- Say the names of the Bible books in which the Bible study is found
- Name and find the four Gospels
- Understand how to read a Bible reference

**Younger children should be introduced to basic information about the Bible and how it is put together.**

Middle Children (Level 2)

Middle children should be able to do everything from Level 1. He should also learn to:

- pronounce the names of the books in the Bible
- locate most Bible books
- use the contents page
- read a Bible reference
- find chapter and verses called for in a reference
- recognize and know the basic groupings of the Old and New Testament books
- identify books with some of the men God used to write the Bible
- identify key books by information contained in them
  —Genesis tells about creation.
  —Exodus tells about Moses.
  —Exodus gives the Ten Commandments.
  —Psalms is the songbook of the Bible.
  —Matthew, Mark, Luke, and John tell about Jesus' life.

*Divisions of the Bible*
**Law**
**History**
**Poetry**
**Major Prophets**
**Minor Prophets**
**Gospels**
**History**
**Paul's Letters**
**General Letters**
**Prophecy**

Preteens (Level 3)

Preteens should be able to do everything from Levels 1 and 2. In addition, when they have completed the sixth grade, they should be able to:

- locate all books in the Bible
- know all the books in order
- read Bible references and locate the Scriptures
- locate a Bible reference and find information from it
- identify and locate certain Bible books according to their content
  —a Bible book that tells about the early church (Acts)
  —a Bible book that tells about the life of Abraham
  —a Bible book that tells of David's early life
- find the names of major Bible people in the books where their stories are recorded
  —Daniel (Daniel)
  —Moses (Exodus)
  —Jesus (Matthew, Mark, Luke, John)
- be able to locate from memory often-used Bible passages and memory verses
  —The Lord's Prayer (Matthew 6, Luke 11)
  —The Ten Commandments (Exodus)
  —The Sermon on the Mount (Matthew 5, Luke 6)
- recognize the basic groupings of the Old and New Testament books and identify all Bible books in those groupings
- recognize the basic divisions of the Old and New Testament books; identify all books in the divisions

## Helping Children Study the Bible

In addition to memory verses and Bible skills, girls and boys are able to study the Bible in other ways. Telling a Bible story in a narrative style, where the leader uses an open Bible and tells the Bible story in her own words, is a time-honored way of presenting the Bible to children. This approach, while enjoyable and suitable to any age, is particularly good for younger children (six and seven year olds). The younger child can be easily engaged in a story such as Jesus' birth and life, stories of Paul's journeys, of Daniel, David, Ruth, Elijah, and Elisha. A Bible narrative can also be presented as an interview, a dialogue, a full-blown drama, or a television production. An adult or child may present a monologue. The children themselves can present the Bible material in pantomime or picture posing.

**A great variety of engaging and interesting Bible narratives are available to be told to children in a narrative manner.**

Guidelines for telling a Bible story follow.

- *Study the story in the Bible.* Know the story so well that you can teach from an overflow of knowledge.
- *Practice telling the story.* Use adjectives, adverbs, and action verbs.
- *Tell the story in your own words.*
- *Hold a Bible open to the passage where the story is found.*
- *Maintain eye contact with children.* Sit where you can see all the girls and boys and they can comfortably see you.
- *Speak clearly and loudly enough to be heard.*
- *Pace the story.*
- *Communicate the emotions of the story.*
- *Involve the children.* Relate the facts of the story to your audience. "Samuel was about your age."
- *Use a variety of storytelling techniques.* Add music, sound effects, or costumes.

**Children's curriculum offers many different ways of presenting the Bible material in narrative form.**

**Speak more slowly or more quickly to indicate the action or "feel" of the story.**

**How did God feel? (Angry); How did the missionaries feel? (Afraid)**

### Bible Search and Study

A second approach to Bible study is the search and study approach generally suitable for older children. Children, working alone or in groups, locate Bible verses and passages and discuss their meaning. They may have present-day situations to which they will find answers in the session's Bible material and related verses.

### Bible Application Narrative

A third approach is the Bible application narrative. Many passages in the Bible, such as those found in Paul's letters, Psalms, and Proverbs, contain truths that girls and boys need to know. But they are not presented in a narrative form in the Bible. One way to teach such material is to construct a narrative from background material. While this remains a suitable approach for younger children, middle children are ready for a more indepth approach. So the message may be presented as a Bible application narrative.

**A Bible application narrative is a combination of the truth in the session Bible passage combined with an appropriate present-day story.**

Using the Bible truth found in the session, the writer constructs a present-day situation in which the characters struggle with that truth in their own lives. For example, the Bible truth is "God wants us to obey Him." A writer presents a story of two children who are in a situation that calls for them to obey their parents. One child does; one doesn't. Through the telling of the story and the discussion of it, children are exposed to what the Bible truth means in their own lives as well as the lives of the children in the story.

**The entire session is a Bible study.**

# Study Plan

This study plan is arranged in ten 15-minute segments so that training may be offered in leader meetings or other occasions when time is short and training could be offered.

The entire plan conducted at one time is designed for a two and one-half hour period. You may need to make some choices when you deal with the methods chapters. In that case, choose what you feel your workers need most.

A worker studying on her own may read the book and complete the "Hands On" activities.

## GENERAL PREPARATION
1. Read the book and the study plan. As you prepare for each segment, review the chapters noted.
2. Provide a copy of the book for each leader or make copies of the activities.
3. Have available markers, pencils, construction paper, writing paper, and other supplies needed to do activities.
4. For sessions seven through ten, make sure yu have all the material for the activities.

## Session I–Chapters 1 and 5
### PREPARE
1. Use "Hands On" activities on pages 10, 12.
2. Make a poster of the five principles of Sunday School Leadership (pp. 58-62).
### TEACH
1. Guide each leader to paper tear a name tag in the initial of her first name. Guide her to write on the name tag her name and one word to describe why she teaches children.
2. Ask leaders to complete "Hands On" activity on page 10.
3. Talk about the purpose of Jesus' teaching.
4. Assign five groups to each read about one of the principles. Guide groups to write the definition on the poster.
5. Point out information on pages 54-57.

## Session 2–Chapters 2 and 3
### PREPARE
1. Use "Hands On" activities on pages 20, 26, and 39.
2. Prepare five strip posters, one for each of the areas of growth.
3. Prepare a poster of Luke 2:52. Place on wall
4. Print one of each of the eight intelligences on eight pieces of construction paper.
### TEACH
1. Give leaders an option of activities on pages 20 and 26. Ask them to keep in mind that child throughout the session.
2. Point out the Luke 2:52 poster. Guide group to repeat the verse together.
3. Present highlights from pages 21-27.
4. Hand out the construction paper titles to eight persons. Guide them to read and share the information from pages 38-39.
5. Guide leaders to do activitiy on page 39.

## Session 3–Chapter 4
### PREPARE
1. Plan to use activities on pages 46, 47, 48, and 53.
### TEACH
1. Guide leaders to do activitiy on page 46.
2. Assign leaders to two groups. Ask each group to complete activity on pages 47-48.
3. Present information on pages 49-52. Guide leaders to do activity on page 53.
4. Close by reading John 13:34-35.

## Session 4–Chapter 6
### PREPARE
1. Plan to use activities on page 75.
2. Have copies of curriculum or sample lessons available to use.
3. Print on three cards: Prepare, Encounter, Continue, one word per card.
### TEACH
1. Assign leaders to three groups. Give each group 1 card. Guide them to examine the

information on pages 71-72. Ask them to make a poster of what they discover. Guide groups to share. Comment or correct.

2. Distribute curriculum and guide leaders to do activity on page 75.

## Session 5–Chapter 7
### PREPARE
1. On three strips print "Real Experiences," Simulations," and "Learning Centers." Place on wall in three different locations.
2. Place large sheets of paper and markers in each area.

### TEACH
1. Guide leaders to join a group. Direct them to the appropriate information in chapter 7 and ask them to prepare a skit presenting what they learn to the larger group.
2. Point out the importance of teaching the children with appropriate methods. Mention the "Exploration Station" materials available in some leader packs.
3. Close by reading Romans 15:4.

## Session 6–Chapter 8 (Research Workshop)
### PREPARE
1. On two strips print "Maps" and "Time Lines." Place on wall in two different locations.

### TEACH
1. Guide leaders to choose one of the two areas and begin work.
2. Point out the benefits of doing research activities with children.

## Session 7–Chapter 9 (Art Workshop)
### PREPARE
1. Prepare these areas: drawing, painting, scenes, and mobiles.
2. From pages 109-113, make copies of the definitions of several types of art. Place the definitions and art supplies in that area.

### TEACH
1. Guide leaders to choose an area in which to work. Encourage them to choose an area with which they are unfamiliar.
2. Give leaders time to share their work. Present information on the significance to children's learning of teaching through art activities. Encourage leaders to offer a variety as they plan for each session.

## Session 8–Chapter 9 (Drama Workshop)
### PREPARE
1. Provide several copies of leader and learner materials. Provide costumes if they are easily available.
2. Make copies of definitions of types of drama from pages 115-116. Place around room.

### TEACH
1. Guide leaders to choose an area in which to work. Suggest they choose a method they have not tried or feel uncomfortable with. Circulate and give help as needed.
2. Give leaders time to share their dramas.
3. Point out the importance of offering a variety of drama activities.

## Session 9–Chapter 10 (Music, Creative Writing Workshop)
### PREPARE
1. Provide several copies of leader and learner materials. Provide simple musical instruments if available. Provide writing materials.
2. Make copies of definitions of types of music and creative writing from pages 120-122 and 124-129. Place in work areas around room.

### TEACH
1. Guide leaders to choose an area. Circulate among groups to encourage and give help.
2. If there is time, encourage groups and individuals to share their work.
3. Point out the importance of offering both music and creative writing learning activities.

## Session 10–Chapters 10 and 11 (Learning Games and Bible Study Workshop)
### PREPARE
1. Find several learning games in outdated resource kits/leader packs. Place them around the room.
2. Prepare to tell a Bible story. Review the guidelines on page 141.
3. Place chairs in a large circle.

### TEACH
1. Direct leaders to spend a few minutes playing games. Debrief.
2. Guide leaders to turn to page 141. Encourage them to watch the guidelines as you present the story. Debrief.
3. Close the session by reading Proverbs 23:12.

# CHRISTIAN GROWTH STUDY PLAN
## FORM - 725 (Rev. 6-99)

NOTE: To receive credit, complete the following form and give to your pastor or another staff person in your church. If you are getting credit for a seminar or conference, give this completed form to your conference or seminar leader.

## CONGRATULATIONS!
### YOU HAVE COMPLETED A COURSE PROVIDED BY THE CHRISTIAN GROWTH STUDY PLAN.

## PARTICIPANT INFORMATION

SOCIAL SECURITY NUMBER (USA ONLY)

PERSONAL CGSP NUMBER*

DATE OF BIRTH (MONTH, DAY, YEAR)

NAME - FIRST, MIDDLE, LAST

HOME PHONE

ADDRESS (STREET, ROUTE, OR P.O. BOX)

CITY, STATE, OR PROVINCE

ZIP/POSTAL CODE

## CHURCH INFORMATION

CHURCH NAME

ADDRESS (STREET, ROUTE, OR P.O. BOX)

CITY, STATE, OR PROVINCE

ZIP/POSTAL CODE

## CHANGE REQUEST ONLY

FORMER NAME

FORMER ADDRESS (STREET, ROUTE, OR P.O. BOX)

CITY, STATE, OR PROVINCE

ZIP/POSTAL CODE

FORMER CHURCH (STREET, ROUTE, OR P.O. BOX)

CITY, STATE, OR PROVINCE

ZIP/POSTAL CODE

## COURSE INFORMATION

Course or Resource Title:

1. The code for this course is ▐▐▐➡

(The course code can be found in the current *Christian Growth Study Plan Catalog*. Your church office can assist you with a catalog.)

2. If the course code begins with "LS (Leadership and Skill)," please check one of the following as appropriate to the ministry area you want to apply this credit. For Code "CG" (Christian Growth), you are automatically enrolled in a subject area diploma plan.

| | | | | |
|---|---|---|---|---|
| 01 ❏ Acteens | 15 ❏ Drama | 28 ❏ Preschool Choir |
| 02 ❏ Adults on Mission | 16 ❏ Evangelism | 30 ❏ Royal Ambassadors |
| 03 ❏ Associational Office Management | 17 ❏ Family Enrichment | 31 ❏ Senior Adult Ministry |
| 44 ❏ Baptist Men On Mission | 18 ❏ Family Ministry | 32 ❏ Single Adult Ministry |
| 05 ❏ Challengers | 19 ❏ Girls in Action | 33 ❏ Special Education |
| 06 ❏ Children's Choir | 20 ❏ Leadership Skill Development | 34 ❏ Stewardship |
| 07 ❏ Children's Choir Coordinator | 21 ❏ Men's Ministry | 35 ❏ Sunday School |
| 08 ❏ Children in Action | 04 ❏ Mission Education | 36 ❏ Weekday Early Educ. Director |
| 45 ❏ Church History Preparation | 23 ❏ Mission Friends | 37 ❏ Weekday Early Educ. Teacher |
| 09 ❏ Church Leadership | 24 ❏ Music Instrumental/Keyboard/Handbell Leader/Performer | 38 ❏ Woman's Enrichment |
| 10 ❏ Church Media | 29 ❏ Mission Kids | 39 ❏ Woman's Missionary Union |
| 11 ❏ Church Recreation | 25 ❏ Music Ministry Leader | 40 ❏ Women on Mission |
| 12 ❏ Church Secretaries | 26 ❏ Music Worship Leaders | 41 ❏ Vocational Preparation |
| 13 ❏ Deacons | 22 ❏ On Mission Team | 42 ❏ Youth Ministers |
| 14 ❏ Discipleship Training | 27 ❏ Pastoral Ministries | 43 ❏ Youth on Mission |

**MAIL THIS REQUEST TO:** CHRISTIAN GROWTH STUDY PLAN
LIFEWAY CHRISTIAN RESOURCES
127 NINTH AVENUE, NORTH
NASHVILLE, TN 37234-0117

SIGNATURE OF PASTOR, TEACHER, OR OTHER CHURCH LEADER

DATE

*New participants are requested but not required to give SS# and date of birth. Existing participants, please give CGSP# when using SS# for the first time. Thereafter, only one ID# is required.